n the East.

10 New Colledge
11 Wadham Colledge
12 Holiwell
13 Vniuersitie Colledge
14 The Phisick Garden Wall
15 Magdalen Bridge ouer Charwell
16 Cittie Walls.

Arms of the Vniuersitie

Balliol Colledge 1263

Exceter Colledge 1316

Queenes Colledge 1340

Lincolne Colledge 1420

Magdalen Colledge 1456

Corpus Christi Colledge 1516

Trinitie Colledge 1556

OXFOR DE

Byene

Gray Fryers
Paradise
Trill gate

the Castle
Prison

Bocardo & Northgate.

ford in the seventeenth century

OXFORD
In the Age of
John Locke

OXFORD
in the Age of
John Locke

W. N. Hargreaves-Mawdsley

NORMAN
UNIVERSITY OF OKLAHOMA PRESS

By W. N. Hargreaves-Mawdsley

A History of Academical Dress in Europe (Oxford, 1963)
A History of Legal Dress in Europe (Oxford, 1963)
The English Della Cruscans and Their Time, 1783–1828 (The Hague, 1967)
A Dictionary of European Writers (London and New York, 1968)
Woodforde at Oxford, 1759–76 (Oxford, 1969)
Spain Under the Bourbons (London and Columbia, S.C., 1972)

Library of Congress Cataloging in Publication Data
Hargreaves-Mawdsley, W   N
    Oxford in the age of John Locke.
    (The Centers of civilization series, v. 32)
    Bibliography: p.
    1. Oxford—History. 2. Oxford. University. 3. Locke, John, 1632–1704. I. Title. II. Series.
DA690.O98H37   914.25'72   72–3598
ISBN 0–8061–1038–4

Copyright 1973 by the University of Oklahoma Press, Publishing Division of the University. Composed and printed at Norman, Oklahoma, U.S.A., by the University of Oklahoma Press. First edition.

To Professor and Mrs. V. H. Galbraith

Oxford friends without peer

Preface

While writing this book, I tried to keep in mind—something not always easy for one so long connected with the City and the University as I was—the remoteness in time and place of seventeenth-century Oxford. It is in fact intended for that increasingly important reader, one to whom more and more (and rightly) the publishing world pays attention, the "general reader," whose interests have broadened as the world has grown smaller.

The question must be answered why I chose the seventeenth century rather than some other period of Oxford's history. I am at home in Oxford's seventeenth-, eighteenth-, and nineteenth-century history, but to me the first of these centuries is the most significant and exciting. Architecturally, scientifically, in its general culture it is among Oxford's brightest periods, and it is also a period during which Oxford as never again was of vast importance in the political history of England, while John Locke, one of the great minds of Europe, headed it, binding together within his mastery so many strands of thinking and of living to be found in the University City at that time.

W. N. HARGREAVES-MAWDSLEY

Brandon, Manitoba, Canada
April 15, 1972

Contents

OXFORD
In the Age of
John Locke

I
Oxford

Oxford as a centre of civilisation needs no apology. The name is known throughout the world, even though only vaguely, and more often than not in connection with the Boat Race. This was particularly the case when England, and I say England rather than Britain, ruled the waves and a good deal of the world during the nineteenth century. It was then that her two universities, Oxford and Cambridge (for the recent foundations of London, Durham, and Manchester had little prestige even at home), not only became fashionable throughout the Empire but were looked upon with fascination in many a foreign land, in France especially.

That was scarcely the case in Germany, where many a herr professor doktor mocked at Benjamin Jowett's reading parties and waxed merry over the lack of research, and there were some at home, some of Oxford themselves, like Matthew Arnold and Mark Pattison, who agreed with them and concluded that the academic future lay in the Reich. The claim of the City as opposed to the University of Oxford to worldwide acknowledgement does not, however, lie in passing fashions nor in social and political trends. It is entrenched behind a tradition spreading away back to distant times when it was the city which was all and when the university was nonexistent. Those who think romantically of Oxford's "dreaming spires" and mourn that they dream seldom nowadays should remember that Town unwillingly received Gown into its bosom and that when it accepted the inevitable the two rubbed shoulders against one another for centuries.

In the Middle Ages the college system was not the rule, but masters and students dwelt in lodgings all over the City and fought with the townsmen in the taverns, and as late as the seventeenth century Robert Burton, of *The Anatomy of Melancholy* fame, bated the bargees till they wept with anger. On St. Scholastica's Day in 1354 a student insulted a vintner and severe riots followed; the University was well in the rough-and-tumble of life. A contemporary account of the trouble vividly presents one with a scene of Town and Gown animosity in the mid-fourteenth century:

"A number of scholars came to the Swyndlestock tavern and there calling for wine, John de Croydon, the vintner brought them some, but they disliking it, as it should seem, and he avouching it to be good, several snappish words passed between them. At length the vintner giving them stubborn and saucy language, they threw the wine and vessel at his head."

Now the townsmen came up promising to stand by him. Long-pent-up jealousy of the University broke loose, and during the next two days students were killed and their hostels looted. Gown was, however, supported by the Crown, and the seal was set on its ascendency by the statutes granted to the University by Edward III in 1375. One can see the illumination on an initial letter in the University Archives with the King, one side of his face drawn down by a paralytic stroke, handing the statutes to the Chancellor of the University. From that time onwards Gown ruled supreme, and it was only in the eighteenth century, as Thomas Hearne the antiquary wryly remarks, that the Mayor began to demur at having to perform in the Church of St. Mary the Virgin an act of obeisance, including the handing over of sixty-three pennies, to the officers of the University every year. Even today the annual Fair of St. Giles, in the heart of the City, cannot begin until formally opened by the Clerks of the Market, who are senior members of the Alma Mater.

The earliest notice of the City of Oxford is that of A.D. 912 in the *Saxon Chronicle*, where it is stated that in that year Edward, the son of Alfred the Great, came into the possession of "London and Oxford and all regions which owed obedience to these cities." Soon afterwards Oxford Castle, the tower of which still stands, was built as part of the defence measures against the Danes. The geographical position of the City, which if one looks at a modern map is today no less striking, was in the troubled days of the tenth century even more vital; for, lying as it did midway between Wessex and Mercia, it was not only in the front line of defense against invasion but also a convenient place for diplomatic activities amidst warring Saxons and Danes. If we are to read between the lines of the references to Oxford in the *Domesday Book*, noticing the great amount of devastation in the area and the work which the Normans undertook to overawe the City and its neighbourhood by the building of fortifications, we must believe that at the Conquest Oxford was the scene of strong opposition to the Normans. Such a tower, built by Robert d'Oyly, Governor of Oxford during William the Conqueror's reign, is still extant, incorporated into the buildings of the Church of St. Michael-at-the-North-gate, and was designed as a watchtower commanding the northerly entrance to the City. The key position which Oxford has, standing as it does astride the Thames, communicating with both the west and central Midlands and within a day's march of London, was next illustrated during the civil war between the supporters of Queen Maud and of King Stephen, which began in 1142. It was there that Maud, driven out of London, held court, and from there that, when besieged by Stephen's army, she escaped across the frozen Thames. It was there that, in 1222, Stephen Langton, Archbishop of Canterbury, held the most important ecclesiastical council ever gathered on English soil, one in fact of European significance. In 1258, Oxford was the scene of the meeting of barons, who, sitting as a parliament, drew up the Provisions of Oxford. Simon de Montfort was the spokesman for the barons, who forced Henry III to accept baronial advice on all occasions.

From then on Oxford began to decline as a city as the Crown became stronger, safely anchored in Westminster, and no barons or pretenders were ready to set up a rival court in Oxford. It was not until the seventeenth century that with the outbreak of the Civil War between Charles I and Parliament history after a long interval repeated itself and the court came to Oxford for refuge. As, however, Oxford the City fell away, Oxford the University gradually came into its own.

As early as about 1130 there are records of schools of all kinds in Oxford with Thibaut of Étampes, Robert Pullein, and the Lombard jurist Vacarius among the masters. The patronage of King Henry I followed, and about this time he had a residence built for himself, Beaumont Palace (commemorated to this day by Beaumont Street), where Richard Coeur de Lion was born in 1157. By now the growing body of masters and scholars was in all but name a *studium generale*. There were thousands of them, living without much discipline all over the town, and these numbers increased still further when, about 1167, Henry II, in his quarrel with Thomas à Becket, prevented further migrations of scholars to Paris, the academic Mecca, and as a result they turned to Oxford.

By the late twelfth century Oxford had become to all intents and purposes a guild of masters. The citizens, however, were none too pleased with this mighty influx of strangers who disrupted their lives and who then, as later, always seemed ready for a street fight, and matters came to a head in 1209, when two students were killed by the townsfolk. This was a much more serious affair than the later one of 1354, already mentioned, for not only

7

scholars but also masters left the town, some of them migrating to Cambridge to form the nucleus of the sister university, whose origin is dated from that year. The ecclesiastical authorities, to prevent a catastrophe leading to the end of a *studium* which was gaining European renown, decided to act, and, though the townsmen were supported by King John, the Church prevailed. In 1214 the Papal Legate drew up the Oxford Ordinance, which granted special rights to the scholars and placed them for centuries in a privileged position beyond the reach of the town. After this there was little to prevent Oxford's *studium* from going on from strength to strength, and it profited from the great crisis in Paris between 1229 and 1231 in gaining further prestige and numbers. By 1250, Henry III had abandoned his bid to control the schools, and the papacy more and more withdrew its direct influence, so that under a series of great chancellors, Robert Grosseteste, Thomas de Chanteloup, Edmund of Canterbury, and Richard de Wyche, who nominally represented the remote Bishop of London, there being no Bishop of Oxford until the Reformation, Oxford gained a degree of independence never enjoyed by Paris, whose Bishop was on the spot.

In 1252, Oxford styled itself a *Universitas*, some time before Paris did, and had the most celebrated schools of canon law and medicine in the civilised world. By 1260, Matthew Paris considered Oxford worthy of being called the rival of Paris, and the seal of its celebrity was set on it when, in 1289, it was granted the title *Studium Generale* by papal bull.

In these early years it was the secular clergy who did the

8

teaching, which was carried on haphazardly with some disruption in houses all over the town and, if there was a lack of such rented buildings, in the side streets. It was during the thirteenth century that the four great orders of mendicant friars, the Dominican (Black) Friars, the Franciscan (Grey) Friars, the Carmelite (White) Friars, and the Augustinian Friars, came to England, being at once attracted to Oxford, and, unlike the older orders of monks, who had taken no part in teaching, threw themselves with enthusiasm into this bracing world. Soon they had built monasteries in Oxford and invited the scholars to them to benefit from their teaching, the quality of which became as a result superior to that found in the secular schools. The latter thereupon lost so many of their adherents that by the fourteenth century the earlier established authorities had a hard fight of it not to lose control over Oxford education. Outstanding among the friars was the almost legendary Roger Bacon (1214–92), who may be said to have established the scientific method, working in the fields of chemistry, astronomy, medicine, and mathematics and discovering, among other things, the properties of lenses.

So successful were these new mendicant orders that the old monastic orders, such as the Benedictines and the Cistercians, began at last to emulate them and, eager to do better than they, started to build conventual schools, so that it was a question not just of inviting the scholars to come to hear the lectures they provided and then depart for their lodgings scattered about the town but of inviting them to live and work within or at least near their monastic buildings. The Benedictines thus built four colleges for this purpose between 1283 and 1435, and the Cistercians to a lesser extent were similarly engaged.

It was this development which led to what for many gives Oxford its particular character, the college system. The authorities, who had always eyed the success of the monks as teachers within the University with jealousy, now decided to adopt their system of master and student communities for themselves. Here was an opportunity to exercise discipline, to gain all the advantages which inter-communication between master and scholar would bring, to say nothing of personal supervision and moral example resulting from a daily contact. It was Walter de Merton who first brought this idea to practical effect, and in 1267 he began to build a college which, with quadrangles, a chapel, and a refectory, was the prototype of all future Oxford colleges. Its statutes, the object of which was to formulate rules for a society of a head, of masters, and of scholars (the first two orders being responsible for the ordering of its property, the rules which were to be observed in the running of it, and the ordering of its studies) were followed more or less by other colleges founded after that time.

By 1525, when Thomas Cardinal Wolsey's foundation (later to become Christ Church) was licensed, ten colleges of a similar character were in existence, and the rules designed for the two greatest foundations of the fifteenth century, All Souls (1438) and Magdalen (1458), were largely based on the Merton original. Merton's two rivals in antiquity, Balliol and University College, whose origins are obscure and which struggled painfully to birth through lack of funds, had gained strength by this time.

John Wycliffe's association with Balliol is noteworthy. A master of University College in the fifteenth century, Edmund Lacy, attended King Henry V at the Battle of Agincourt and directed the attention of his sovereign to the fact that money could be well bestowed on colleges. Exeter in the fourteenth century had already profited from the patronage of Queen Margaret of Anjou, Oriel had had as its patron Edward II, and the royal house of Lancaster was particularly addicted to Queen's.

Already the colleges were showing what scholarship was, and they continued to do so. A list of scholars of European renown whom Oxford was nurturing during the fourteenth and fifteenth centuries would include Thomas Linacre of All Souls; John Wycliffe and John Colet, the latter the founder of St. Paul's School, London, prime example of the grammar schools, both Balliol men; William Grocyn, the finest Latin scholar of his age and the first Oxford teacher of Greek, from whom Erasmus learned that language, calling him his "patronus et praeceptor," educated at Exeter College, although he held his fellowship at New College; and Henry Chichele, Archbishop of Canterbury, one of the earliest fellows of New College, that college having as its founder the great William of Waynflete, Bishop of Winchester, a scholar of European reputation. Merton, ahead of all the rest in age, had nurtured none other than John Duns Scotus himself. And then there was Henry Cardinal Beaufort of Queen's. The secret of the power which Oxford was to exercise in the coming centuries reposes in the statutes drawn up for New College by William of Wykeham on its foundation in 1379. Within its stately buildings, magnificent quadrangle, fine chapel, a great hall nearby, and gardens—indeed all the appurtenances of a noble estate— his scholars, after a training in the liberal arts, were to devote themselves to theology and law with a view to serving Church and State. Oxford in its earlier days had sometimes stood midway between ecclesiastical and secular power, between papal legate and king. It had profited from both; both had wished to gain possession of it, and both had failed. From now on, with the blessing of the University, the colleges of which it was composed trained their members to serve both on their own terms, and in so doing they brought to Oxford a power and influence in the nation's affairs without parallel among the other universities of Europe.

The Renaissance found an eager welcome in Oxford, and in the late fifteenth century her scholars, such as Grocyn, Hugh Latimer, Linacre, and Colet, were returning from Italy zealous for the new learning. Erasmus arrived in 1497 and found the atmosphere of the University, graced as it was by the presence of Thomas More, unequalled by all the European centres of learning which he had visited.

"I found," Erasmus wrote in a letter to a friend, "a most agreeable and wholesome climate; so much politeness, and such profound erudition both in Greek and Latin, that mere curiosity alone takes me to Italy. When I listen to Colet, I think I hear Plato. Who must not admire Grocyn's extensive learning in all the sciences? Who is more profound, more judicious, more penetrating than Linacre? Has nature ever formed a more engaging or more happy disposition than More?—I pass over many in silence. It is surprising how greatly scholarship flourishes here."

The first foundation inspired by the new learning was Corpus Christi College, endowed by Bishop Richard Fox in 1517. Greek was to be a speciality there, and the old scholasticism was, in the spirit of Erasmus and More, to be outfaced. That very year, however, a certain monk, called Martin Luther, was nailing a notice to a door in far away Wittenberg, or, what is probably nearer the truth but less romantic, sending it by post: the Reformation had come into being. Meanwhile, Cardinal Wolsey was busy buying up property for his new college, for which he built a hall and a kitchen so magnificent that there was no money left for a chapel, and the adjacent St. Frideswide's Church had to be pressed into service. Then he suddenly fell from royal favour in 1530, and before long, much against their will, the chancellor and masters of Oxford were drawn into the question of Henry VIII's divorce and so into the English Reformation.

In the complete break with Rome which followed, the University was generally a reluctant spectator. Thomas Cromwell's men descended on it, and before long half the glory of the town was ruined; two abbeys, five friaries, and five monastic colleges vanished, and the western quarter of Oxford, which contained most of its finest buildings, was devastated. Conventual Oxford was razed to the ground, although many treasures were taken to safety in the secular colleges. These survived the first storm, but in the second under Edward VI even these were in great part destroyed; illuminated manuscripts went up in flames, and stained glass and statues which Cromwell, afraid of Henry VIII's waverings and changes of mind, had been unwilling to touch, were ravaged by Edward VI's pitiless commissioner, John Dudley, Earl of Warwick, as "symbols of superstition."

When Mary Tudor brought about a return to Rome, most members of the University supported her, were glad to burn Latimer and Nicholas Ridley at the stake outside Balliol in Broad Street, rejoiced in the new foundations of Trinity and St. John's (1554 and 1555) on the traditional plan, and bowed low to Reginald Cardinal Pole. Then came the death of Mary in 1558, and with the succession of her sister, Elizabeth I, to the English throne the Reformation settled on Oxford for good; but the government acted with caution, and the Visitation of 1559 avoided an aggressive policy. Room was still left for compromise, and in some colleges members of the Old Faith managed for a time to hold their own; but by 1564, when the Earl of Leicester was appointed University Chancellor, the reforming party had gained the upper hand, and he encouraged it. Active and meticulous in his office, Leicester carried out the government's policy of attaching Oxford firmly to the state. Two years later Queen Elizabeth's visit to the University was a triumph; conformity had been achieved. Leicester's chancellorship may be considered the beginning of Oxford's modern era. The matriculation register was started in 1565. The jumble of statutes, some contradictory and dating from the thirteenth century, was put in order, and discipline was enforced on senior and junior members alike.

In order to bind the University more closely still to the Crown, it was incorporated by act of Parliament in 1571.

Undergraduates were forced to live in colleges, and lodgings in the town were frowned on, while for the first time
a large number of students paid their way through the
colleges and were not dependent on scholarships. They
were known as commoners and, if of particular rank and
wealth, as gentlemen-commoners or noblemen.

The comfort of life had improved, and was luxurious
in the eyes of the Puritan party, which was increasingly
in evidence. But for all the outward show, with poetry and
drama in the air—some University dramatic companies
were invited to perform at Court, many a graduate like
George Peele was hurrying away to London to become an
actor, and was not *Hamlet* itself produced in Oxford in
1607, for how could the authorities condemn what the
Court approved?—the old dry-as-dust tradition prevailed
in the schools. Aristotle was still the lodestone, and upon
hearing Ptolemy's system of the universe so much quoted
by academics, one would think that Copernicus had never
existed. If Francis Bacon, a Cambridge visitor granted, is
to be believed, Oxford was at the close of the sixteenth
century rapidly falling behind the times, for in an age of
discovery, when circumnavigation of the globe became a
reality, here were crabbed schoolmen taking Pliny, the
first-century Roman, as the supreme authority on geography.

There was nonetheless something which Bacon did not
mention. Prized to this day by the learned world, the
Bodleian Library came into being in 1598, when Sir
Thomas Bodley began to restore the University Library,
founded by Humfrey, Duke of Gloucester, in 1444 and
subsequently much neglected, many of the books having

been lost and the building become half-ruinous. By the date of Bodley's death in 1612 the library, restored, extended, and filled with treasures, was secure for the future.

The Stuart Age was ushered in by James I, that learned pedant and sampler of theology; and as the King delighted in the unending discourses of the Hampton Court Conference of 1604, thus aggravating an already existing religious hypersensitiveness in the country, so Oxford found itself in the early seventeenth century mired in ecclesiastical controversy. High Churchmanship was coming to the fore, patronised by the Court and by an increasing number of Oxonians; soon it would stand face to face with Puritanism until Crown and Parliament, Divine Right and People's Will, prelate and presbyterian would find themselves on the field of battle. All the same, by the end of the first quarter of the seventeenth century there had been a revival of learning, the undergraduate population had risen to about two thousand, and during this period chairs were founded in philosophy, astronomy, music, history, and geometry. Medicine had been at a discount since the death of Linacre, known not only as a scientist but also as a Greek scholar, in 1524. The University now bestirred itself in this field also, and in emulation of such new and forward-looking universities as Leyden a physic garden was laid out, in which could be grown every kind of herb with a medicinal property. The arrival in Oxford in 1642 of William Harvey, discoverer of the circulation of the blood, only seemed to confirm its scientific reputation.

A new chapter in the University's history had begun in 1630, when William Laud, Archbishop of Canterbury, became Chancellor. Not since Leicester had there been such a head, and there was not to be another in the following centuries. Laud represented the move of the High Church, in alliance with the Court, against the Puritans; for Oxford he represented authority and discipline. His University meant a great deal to him, and he realised that its fortunes were at the crossroads, that Leicester's chancellorship and the very character of the extrovert Elizabethan Age, with its inclination towards extravagance and its invitation to the "gilded youth" to spend a few years of dilettante idleness in its midst, had damaged it. Oxford must be reformed, although tenderly, in accordance with the requirements of an era with rapidly expanding horizons and growing contacts with Europe.

With increasing competition from Italy, now flowering into a second if much feebler Renaissance and more accessible to travellers than ever before, and the Netherlands rejoicing in their newfound freedom, Oxford must hold its head the highest of all. Laud's remarkable revision of the statutes resulted in the Laudian Codex of 1636, which remains the basis of the laws of the University to this day. In it Laud may be said to have revived the principles of learning and sobriety which governors and benefactors of the past had kept before them as the polestar of their aims. The whole system of ruling the University was reviewed, and by matching apparent inconsistencies and paring away excrescences it was made more efficient, while courses of study, freed from the strait jacket of lingering mediaeval convention, were made elastic enough to absorb new demands. In that year, when the Codex was published and the Archbishop lavishly

17

entertained King Charles I in his newly built Italianesque inner quadrangle at St. John's, Laudian Oxford stood at its height.

When a few years later the Civil War broke out, Charles I went to Oxford as a safer capital—he knew that it was loyal to Church and Crown—bringing his army and his court with him. The King settled in Christ Church, the great college which Henry VIII had refounded after Wolsey's fall, while Charles's ministers of state were scattered round the various colleges. The Royalists made free with all that Oxford willingly gave them, and the kitchens buzzed and the cellars were ransacked to please the visitors. A mint was set up for the issue of a royal coinage of the realm, and for this and any other cause the colleges made over their wealth of silver to the King. Troops clanked through quadrangles and gardens, elbowed doctors of divinity and consequential merchants off the pavements of High Street, and at night they took their noisy pleasures in the numerous taverns. The antiquary John Aubrey relates in his *Miscellanies* (1696) how as an Oxford freshman in 1642 he "was wont to go to Christ Church, to see King Charles I at supper; when I once heard him say, That as he was hawking in Scotland, he rode into the quarry, and found the covey of partridges falling upon the hawk; and I do remember this expression further, viz.' and I will swear upon the book 'tis true.' When I came to my chamber, I told this story to my tutor; said he, *that covey was London*."

It was at this time that Charles, as was then still the custom, consulted a great folio Virgil in the Bodleian for the *"sortes Vergilianae"*—Virgil had been considered a wizard in the Middle Ages—eager to know of his future, closing his eyes, turning the pages, and letting his finger rest pointing to a certain line. The one at which that finger rested referred to Dido's imprecation that the body of King Aeneas would lie headless and unburied on a lonely shore. We can see the grave faces in Duke Humfrey's Library, the figures amidst the gloom of books and panelling. Undergraduates broke off from work and helped to dig the fortification ditches; the old walls were strengthened and manned day and night. Cannons were drawn up around the City (it had now had its own cathedral and bishop for more than a hundred years), the pleasant open land stretching down to the River Cherwell from that time being called The Parks— not to describe what we call a park, but after the term gun parks, or gun emplacements. Lectures became fewer and fewer, gowns were less and less often seen in the streets. The Parliamentary army drew inexorably round Oxford, and in April, 1646, King Charles escaped while there was still time.

That was the beginning of the end for the Royalists, and when Oliver Cromwell visited Oxford, he came as Chancellor with Puritan commissioners round his heels, sworn to the purging of Oxford from "malignants," as they termed the Royalists. All heads of colleges were removed excepting three, and many fellows lost their places; but thanks to the moderating influences of some, noteworthily John Wilkins, Warden of Wadham, who, as discussed later, may be said to have gathered together the nucleus of the Royal Society, by the 1650's prosperity, if not complete normality of academic life, was returning.

When therefore in 1652 John Locke entered Christ Church, it was into a University community which, fast recovering, contained within it men famous in philosophy and the sciences: Thomas Sydenham, the physician; Jonathan Goddard, the first Englishman to make a telescope; John Wallis, who had worsted Hobbes in philosophical controversy; and a wealthy visitor from London, Robert Boyle. Christopher Wren (1632–1723), although the same age as Locke, had already graduated and was an All Souls fellow.

Now why should Locke be chosen to give his name to an age of Oxford? Would not Wren have been suitable, for example, or are there not others who would do as well? Perhaps it is enough to say that Locke by his manifold interests not only mirrored the great variety and activities of the University of his own day but also by his political thought, which spread over Europe from the end of the seventeenth century and, inspiring Montesquieu and Voltaire and Rousseau, conditioned the climate which led to the French Revolution. Locke opposed arbitrary government and authoritarianism in religion; he welcomed the new science and brought principles of scientific criticism to bear on even the most hallowed texts. In his adherence to concrete experience, being indifferent to abstract speculation and suspicious of "mystical enthusiasm," he can fitly be said to have initiated the Age of Reason. Thus he is the typical Oxonian of his age, with even wider interests than Wren, and an intellectual who, inspired by many intellectual facets of the European scene, lived to influence it as no other Englishman of his era save the Cantabrigian Isaac Newton.

John Locke (1632–1704), whose father was steward to a landowner, was educated at Westminster and came up to Oxford in 1652. He seems to have been chiefly distinguished in his undergraduate years for an "ingenious epigram" on Cromwell's peace with the Dutch in 1653. Five years later, having taken his master's degree, he turned to the study of medicine, and, although he did not take a medical degree until 1675, he had patients, one of whom by mere chance was the famous Whig politician Anthony Ashley-Cooper, afterwards First Earl of Shaftesbury. This meeting brought him into touch with the political world, in which he followed his patron's fortunes. Meanwhile he took a leading part as student (that is, fellow) of Christ Church in the intellectual life of Oxford, being one of the first to teach the new philosophy of Descartes in place of Aristotelianism. As Francis Wrangham was to write in his quaint "Life of John Locke" in *The British Plutarch* (1795), "[Cartesianism] had indeed been for some time universally taught in Holland, and at Geneva, and had captivated many others, as well as Mr. Locke, with the charming variety and perspicuity of the style in which the founder had dressed it up."

Locke eagerly joined the group which gathered round Robert Boyle, the great physicist and chemist, whose own particular contribution to science at this time was his pioneering work on meteorology. By 1670, Locke had begun to sketch out a draft of his *Essay Concerning Human Understanding*, and from that time onwards he was constantly in touch with the broader field of London.

In the variety of his interests Locke illustrates the

universality of the scholars of his age, and as much as any-one he made Oxford intellectualism widely known in Europe. He was praised for his scientific knowledge by such great authorities as Thomas Sydenham in England and Peter Guenelon in Amsterdam, while in Montpellier, France, he was regarded as an authority on law, and he was acclaimed by such French Protestant theologians as Toignard. The finest epitaph to Locke is perhaps to be found in *Vindication of the Political Principles of Mr. Locke* (1782) , by Joseph Towers. There Towers summed up as well as anyone the significance of Locke in the eyes of his widest public:

"Mr. Locke's treatise on government was calculated to increase the liberty of mankind, and to place them in a situation of greater dignity and felicity, than had been afforded them by the various systems of tyranny and oppression, which have taken place under the name of government, in the different ages and nations of the world. . . . He laboured to elucidate the Sacred Scriptures, to advance the interests of revelation and of virtue, to loosen the bands of tyranny, and to promote the cause of liberty, of justice, and of humanity. . . . The sentiments of Mr. Locke are founded upon reason, truth and justice; and his name will continue to be reverenced wherever learning, liberty, and virtue, shall be held in estimation."

For our purpose, however, it is the Locke of Oxford who counts, the man of wide culture, of tolerant spirit, and of scientific enquiry, Oxford's fitting balance to Isaac Newton at Cambridge, the one quietly active in the world, the other grandly abstracted, both to become the fathers of Europe's fundamental revolution at the end of the following century.

Lastly, what was it like, the Oxford to which Locke came in 1652? Let us approach it from London, from the east. Reaching the crest of Headington Hill, we see gentle slopes with cattle grazing fall to rich water meadows and descend past scattered private houses with trim gardens stretching out behind them. We are in the parish of St. Clement's, whose church with its squat tower stands sentinel on the left. The road narrows to a long, low bridge of many piers and arches, with the River Cherwell meandering below the pollarded willows. We pass on our left the noble avenues of Magdalen Walks, and then, as we leave the East Bridge and the thoroughfare broadens into the width of High Street, the grey perpendicular splendour of Magdalen with its soaring tower rises on our left. Now houses with long, fully sloping eaves intervene before we pass through the low-arched East Gate with a guardian watchtower, and we are inside the City walls, which stretch away to right and left, low and battlemented with turrets at intervals, Longwall Street to our right, before we find ourselves travelling between higher, richer-looking houses, behind which to the right peeps the tower of St. Peter's-in-the-East and trees innumerable. Queen's stands back from the street on our right, masked by cottages, but on our left the front of University College comes right down to it. As High Street curves gently left before it settles into its clean sweep to Carfax, there are more surprises in store. All Souls faces the High but stretches away to the right half the length of Catte Street, noble and austere without, of course, the Hawksmoor towers and other embellishments of the eighteenth century. Now to our left come the humble buildings of St. Mary Hall, quaintly straggling (that frontage to be wrenched down in the early twentieth century to make way for the impertinences of the Rhodes Building, the little hall being recklessly absorbed into Oriel). On our right is St. Mary-the-Virgin's Church, for long the centre of all University affairs and still that of its religion, its spire the most beautiful monument of the Decorated style in the city. More houses with shops among them lie on both sides of the way, and then on the right high-pitched All Saints' Church with its lofty clerestory and narrow tower with a stump of a steeple (not the one we see today, which was rebuilt in 1708 to a design by that amateur architect and composer of glees, jolly Dean Henry Aldrich of Christ Church).

More neat house fronts, their variously sloping roofs a delight to the eye, and then we are at Carfax (Quatre Fours), the crossroads of the City, with a delicate Italianesque conduit in the middle. We turn right, glimpsing as we turn South Street (now St. Aldate's), in the distance the tower of Wolsey's dining hall at Christ Church, and then, as we swing round St. Martin's Church (of which today only the tower remains), we turn into the Cornmarket, with its covered stalls in the middle of the street, and so out by the North Gate with the sentinel tower Bocardo, as old as the Conquest, on the right.

We are outside the walls again. But there would have been much more to see: the wide avenue of St. Giles's with its two churches, St. Mary Magdalene and St. Giles's, one at either end, with St. John's, taking pride of place, on its eastern side; Broad Street with Balliol (a very different one from what we now see), with a "fender"—an enclosure of trees with a lawn standing out into the street in front of it—and with a garden-locked Trinity College engulfed in trees, having only a narrow lane for egress, to the side of it; wonderful above all the pinnacles of New College in Holywell Parish on the northeast, though still within the walls; and, so that no part of the City should be without some jewel, Merton with its tower.

Elsewhere one would remark on the Divinity School, one of the finest Perpendicular buildings of all time, and the Schools Tower, a cause for wonder in Locke's day, and symptomatic of the taste of his age, that age when Italy put the Gothic to flight.

The above description is based on Wenceslas Hollar's map of 1643. Soon, led on by Christopher Wren, the Italianised Classic would prevail, and Locke's Oxford would present in its new buildings a style of architecture, which, whether one appreciates it or not, must be acknowledged as a style without parallel in the world. But of that later.

In this setting Locke and his contemporaries lived, within a walled and gated city, a small city with fields, gardens, and rivers close by; with muddy, unpaved streets; with wains rolling in with market produce; a city of bells and of silences, of the cry of the watchman at night and higglers during the day; a city of taverns. Everywhere the cap and gown was seen as the University pursued its way, an academic society, its character formed by a strange compromise, one of which English history is so full, its senior members consisting of the clergy of an urbane form of Protestantism, bound to celibacy for so long as they enjoyed their college's patrimony.

Far away west of the City, raised high on its siege works, stood d'Oyly's Castle, alone and half-forgotten. The symbol of the townsmen was no longer the focal point, while the Town Hall was a small building of no account. The Gown had completely driven the Town into submission. At times the fights outside the taverns, dispersed by the gowned proctors, showed on the one hand the resentment of the townsmen and on the other the contempt of the robe for the unlettered. Indeed, the Vice-Chancellor can bring citizens to trial: the University is in control. Nevertheless the people of Oxford live on; the tradesmen work as before—coopers, chandlers, bellowsmakers, silversmiths, coachbuilders, farriers, bakers, college servants—certainly the high thinkers are dependent on them. The shopkeeper often owns a very pleasant dwelling place up a flight of stairs over his business. The lives of Town and Gown are intertwined, and the mayors who come and go can rest assured that the City is a corporation hallowed by time and that, in the words of the Statute of King Henry IV of 1407, referring to Oxford, "The great Charter, and the Charter of the Forest, and all other good Statutes made before this Time, and not repealed, stand in their force."

II

Oxford's Inner World

How did Town and Gown live in Locke's day? Anthony
à Wood (1632–95) of Merton College, part devoted antiquary, part gossipmonger, who lived out his lonely life
between his rooms in Merton Street and his college across
the way, left in his diaries and other papers an unrivalled
account of Oxford life during what Andrew Clark, his
devoted editor, described as "that stormy half-century,
1640–90," Locke's in fact. Of course, these diaries do not
constitute Wood's chief claim to serious authorship. In
spite of what might be inferred from his malicious gossip
and his odds and ends gathered from the byways of erudition, he yet had definite ideas about research and the
scholar's duties and carried them out. Every Oxford historian must honour him for his *History of Oxford down*

to 1640, on which he was engaged until 1674, and for his *Athenae Oxonienses* and *Fasti Oxonienses,* on which from 1680 onwards he was stubbornly at work amid the trials of increasing deafness, trouble with his brother and sister-in-law who kept house for him, snubs ending in outright enmity from university officials, and persecution at the hands of the Second Earl of Clarendon, High Steward of the University.

In Wood's diaries much comes to life. In his papers we see the college halls, where charcoal fires burned and where before the Restoration of 1660 all the social life of the colleges occurred. Here took place the "fresh nights," when freshmen were "initiated" to the accompaniment of "buffooning speeches" and when the new undergraduates had to undergo such indignities as having to quaff salted beer, called "salting them." We seem to see the beautiful silver grace cup handed round at High Table among the fellows, which was the signal for concluding meals, and the undergraduates rising as they passed down the hall. The hours of meals are noted: The day began with the "morning draught" of college beer brewed on the premises (Queen's continued to produce its own until World War II) . Then came breakfast in hall at 9:00 A.M., dinner in hall at 11:00 A.M., bread and beer as a snack in mid-afternoon, and supper in hall at 6:00 P.M. After the Restoration common rooms were started. There masters of arts were able to take their ease in private instead of round the fire in hall, and so popular did they become that by 1678, Wood notes, the senior men spent "whole afternoons" in them, that is, till 5:00 P.M., when the coffeehouses in the City opened.

As for rooms in college, the general arrangement was that of a "chamber," which meant a large living and sleeping room shared by two or more undergraduates, with some small closets in which they did their reading, hence the continual references to "chamber fellows." There were entertainments, such as that at the reception of a new head of a college; on the occasion of the admission of the proctors, who were in charge of university discipline; and those called "gaudies," when specially good dinners were given and guests from outside the colleges were entertained. There were feasts of various kinds on such thanksgiving days as those celebrating the discovery of the Gunpowder Plot and the king's birthday. It was the age of bonfires, sometimes spontaneous, sometimes ordered by the Court, sometimes held in the quadrangle, sometimes lit in the street—with what disorder may be well imagined.

We read of punishments ranging from deprivation of a fellowship to whipping of an undergraduate. Sometimes a prostitute or a beggar was literally driven from Oxford, accompanied often enough by sympathetic junior members. There were sad occasions when epidemics struck the City, and those with infectious diseases were boarded out of college with an apothecary or a physician or in the house of a college servant. From time to time the doleful sound of the passing bell was heard through the mists of that low-lying countryside between two rivers, bringing news of the death of a member of a college. Processions there were in abundance, the doctors in their scarlet "formalities" making a brave show.

Although public concerts were much frowned upon

and theatricals were sternly forbidden, there were many private "music meetings," at which rounds, madrigals, and catches were sung, and sackbuts (trombones), trumpets, pipes, oboes, viols, violins, and lutes were played. As readers of Thomas Hearne, Wood's counterpart in eighteenth-century Oxford, will know, subscription concerts came into their own in the next-but-one generation, when the Holywell Music Room was built, the first public music room in Europe, and Handel made several successful visits to the City.

It was outwardly a slow and ceremonious age, and the long and voluminous gowns, worn always by members of the University even on country walks (and illustrated in a series of copper engravings by George Edwards, collected in 1674 as *Omnium Ordinum Habitumque Academicorum Exemplaria*), are symbolic of the time. University ceremonies culminating in the "Act," or "Encaenia," held in July, were the envy of Cambridge and various foreign universities. The Act proper meant the final, if mostly formal, exercises for the degrees of master of arts and doctor of divinity, law, or medicine. Up to 1664 the Act was held in St. Mary-the-Virgin's Church, and then, after four years without such an act, it took place at the opening of the Sheldonian Theatre, built by Christopher Wren (one of his first creations), and paid for by Gilbert Sheldon (1598–1677), Archbishop of Canterbury and one-time Warden of All Souls. Let John Evelyn (1620–1706), famed diarist and good friend of Oxford, who was present at the opening of the Sheldonian, receiving an honorary Doctorate of Civil Law, describe the Act:

"7 July, 1669. I went towards Oxford; lay at Little

Wycomb. — 8. Arrived at Oxford. — 9. In the morning was celebrated the Encenia of the New Theater, so magnificently built by the munificence of Dr. Gilbert Sheldon, Abp. of Canterbury, in which was spent £25,000, as Sir Christopher Wren, the architect, (as I remember) told me; and yet it was never seene by the benefactor, my Lord Abp., having told me that he never did nor ever would see it. It is in truth a fabrick comparable to any of this kind of former ages, and doubtless exceeding any of the present. . . . To the Theater is added the famous Sheldonian Printing-house. This being at the Act and the first time of opening the Theater (Acts being formerly kept in St. Mary's church, which might be thought indecent, that being a place set apart for the immediate worship of God, and was the inducement for building this noble pile) it was now resolv'd to keep the present Act in it, and celebrate its dedication with the greatest splendor and formalitie that might be, and therefore drew a world of strangers and other companie to the University from all parts of the nation. The Vice Chancellor, Heads of Houses, and Doctors, being seated in magisterial seates, the Vice Chancellor's chaire and deske, Proctors, &c. covered with Brocatall [a kind of brocade] and cloth of gold; the Universitie Register [Registrar] read the founder's grant and gift of it to the Universitie for their scolastic exercises upon these solemn occasions. Then follow'd Dr. South, the Universitie's Orator, in an eloquent speech, which was very long, and not without some malicious and indecent reflections on the Royal Society, as underminers of the University, which was very foolish and untrue, as well as unseasonable. But, to let that pass from an ill natur'd man, the rest was in praise of the Archbishop and the ingenious architect. This ended, after loud musiq from the corridor above, where an organ was plac'd, there follow'd divers panegyric speeches both in prose and verse, interchangeably pronounc'd by the young students place'd in the rostrums, in Pindarics, Eclogues, Heroics, &c. mingled with excellent musiq, vocal and instrumental, to entertain the ladies and the rest of the company. A speech was then made in praise of academical learning. This lasted from 11 in the morning till 7 at night, which was concluded with ringing of bells and universal joy and feasting."

The Act lasted for three days. "Act Saturday" consisted of the "music-lecture," certain disputations called vesperies (*Vesperiae*), a speech by a *terrae filius* (a licensed University buffoon) chosen from among the undergraduates who was free to make personal attacks on his seniors —a cause for embarrassment—and the "Vesper Supper." Next day was "Act Sunday," when the University sermons were preached in St. Mary's by those who were about to take degrees in divinity. On "Act Monday" public disputations (in the mediaeval sense of two candidates for a degree arguing against one another with much Aristotelian jargon with a professor in charge) were held. These were known as the *Comitia* and were followed by more speeches, after which the creation of masters and doctors took place.

After this ceremony (and here again the influence of the Middle Ages leaks through) the proceedings degenerated into an entertainment with actors, ropedancers, and jugglers appearing on a platform "as at a fair," this being the only occasion on which such people were allowed into Oxford. It is frequently mentioned by contemporaries how much more learned were the Acts in Puritan times and how well in hand the *terrae filii* were kept then. Although in Wood's day their often filthy speeches led to the expulsion of the undergraduates, yet remarkably enough the "office" was not abolished for many years.

Two men give us a particular insight into the state of mind and the intellectual climate of Oxford in the Age of Locke. The first is Stephen Penton (1635?–1706), Principal of St. Edmund Hall, whose quaint book, *The Guardians Instructor; or, The Gentlemans Romance*, appeared in 1688. In this satire a father, whose career at Oxford was cut short by the outbreak of the Civil War between Charles I and Parliament (and whose experience of the University before that was none too good) , is persuaded by a neighbouring clergyman to send his second son to his Alma Mater. Armed with a letter of introduction from the worthy cleric, the father journeys to Oxford with his family and seeks out his son's destined tutor in college. Instead of welcoming him, the tutor creates all kinds of difficulties and makes Oxford life sound so strict that, according to the father, "my boy clung about his mother and cry'd to go home again." The fact is that the lazy tutor wants no more charges in his care; he prefers to enjoy the common room undisturbed. In the rules that he outlines as those to be observed during an undergraduate's career, we do, however, in the midst of the satire gain a glimpse of Oxford life in Locke's time. First of all, says the tutor, the student must obey the rules of his college down to the very letter; moreover, he must study hard for five years, and he must stay at the University for the whole of his first year without going home.

Warming to his subject, the tutor continues that the undergraduate must not frequent *"public places* such as are bowling greens, racket courts, etc. for beside the danger of firing his blood by a *fever*, heightening passion into *cursing* and *swearing*, he must unavoidably grow acquainted with promiscuous company, whether they are or are not *vertuous...."*

"Be sure," the tutor continues, "that he discharge all dues *quarterly*, and not learn to run into debt, this will make him gain credit and buy cheaper...." "Whatever letters of *complaints* he writes home," he warns, "I desire you to send me a copy...." "I understand," he goes on, "... that you have brought him up a *fine padd* to keep here for his health's sake; now I will tell you the use of an horse in *Oxford*, and then do as you think fit. The horse must be kept at an *ale-house* or an *inn,* and he must have leave to go once *every day* to see him eat oats, because the master's eye makes him fat; and it will not be *genteel* to go often to an house and spend nothing; and then there may be some danger of the horse growing *resty* if he be not used often, so that you must give him leave to go to *Abingdon* once every week to look out of the tavern window, and see the maids sell turnips...."

After the tutor has continued to burden the father with rules for his son about attending the University Church, about his money allowance, about his choice of friends, and about the books he should read, the poor parent invites the tutor to dinner at his inn, "but he refused, saying that such houses were not built for *gown-men*, and made me leave my son to dine with him, having (said he) observed the great *improvidence* of the gentry, who when they come to enter a son, . . . bring *wife* and *daughters* to shew them the university: there's mighty feasting and drinking for a week, every tavern examin'd, and all this with the company of a child, forsooth, sent up hither for *sobriety* and *industry*. After this he invited us the next day to a Commons; and according to his *humour* before, I expected to have been *starved* in his chamber, and the girles drank chocolette at no rate in the morning for fear of the *worst*. It was very pleasant to see when we came, the *constrain'd* artifice of an unaccustomed complement; silver tankards heaped upon one another; napkins, some twenty years younger than the rest; glasses fit for a *Dutchman* at an *East-India Return*."

There is no such playful satire in the *Private Memoirs of John Potenger, Esq.*, by John Potenger (1647–1733) of Corpus Christi College. Here we have a serious account of the curriculum followed in the third quarter of the seventeenth century. Potenger was elected a scholar of Corpus, having had excellent supporting letters from such influential persons as the Bishop of Winchester and having successfully passed a test in translating Horace and Lucius Florus (he was forgiven his weakness in Greek as being very young). He was assigned to an excellent tutor, who "did not only endeavour to make his pupils good scholars, but good men."

"I did not immediately enter upon logick and philosophy," writes Potenger, "but was kept for a full year to the reading of classical authors, and making theams in prose and verse. . . . At dinner and supper, it being the custom to speak latin, my words were few, till I came to a toller- able proficiency in colloquial latin. My tutor Mr. Roswell, was so pleased with several of my performances in latin, and english verse, that he gave me several books for an encouragement. I acquired just logick and philosophy enough to dispute in my turn in the hall, for I was addicted most to poetry, and making of declamations, two exer- cises I desired to excell in. . . . Being about twenty years of age, the time drew nigh for me to go out Bachelour of Arts, and in order to that, I did my publick exercises in the schools, and my private in the college. . . . The last two years I stayed in the university, I was Bachelour of Arts, and I spent most of my time in reading books, which were not very common, as Milton's Works, Hobbs his Leviathan; but they never had the power to subvert the principles which I had received, of a good christian, and a good subject."

Plenty of work was certainly done, and, as will later be discussed, the second half of the seventeenth century in Oxford was a time of thought and of experimentation in what was then known as natural philosophy, which paved the way for the Age of Reason in the following century. It is here of interest to note that there was no division between arts and sciences and that "moral" philosophers and "natural" philosophers rubbed shoulders in the Royal Society. Indeed, men like Sir Kenelm Digby, John Evelyn, and Samuel Pepys, and for that matter King Charles II and Prince Rupert, were men who loved books, music, and the fine arts—many of them practitioners in some art, authors often too—and who at the same time were keen amateur scientists.

Oxford University in Locke's day contained many men with such varied interests living in an atmosphere of expectancy and optimism, and what in the nineteenth century became unfortunately rival worlds of arts and science were all one. In Anthony à Wood's pages we find references to such studies as anatomy (classes in which, given by an Italian, were eagerly attended in April, 1692), architecture, chemistry, "the globes," mathematics and optics. As for the traditional disciplines there is much mention in Wood of canon and civil law, logic, and rhetoric. Not that there were not opponents of the new pursuits, and at the time of the opening of the Ashmolean Museum (the one in Broad Street, not to be confused with the Fine Arts Museum in Beaumont Street, which belongs to a later time), Wood notes in 1683: "Many are delighted with new phil[osophies] are taken with them; but some, for the old [that is, moral philosophy], look upon them as ba[u]bles. Ch[rist] Ch[urch] men not there. . . ." That is that Christ Church, the headquarters of theology, looked askance at the new enterprise. Such, however, formed the minority. Unfortunately Christ Church was Locke's college, and he lived among intellectual aliens who many years later caused his Oxford downfall.

The new academic climate of Oxford was well illustrated by three entries in John Evelyn's diary. On July 12, 1654, he noted: "We went to St John's, saw the library and the two skeletons, which are finely cleansed and put together; observable is here also the store of mathematical instruments, chiefly given by the late Archbishop Laud, who built here a handsome quadrangle. . . . Hence to the Physic Garden, where the sensitive plant was showed us for a great wonder. There grew canes, olive-trees, rhubarb, but no extraordinary curiosities, besides very good fruit, which, when the ladies had tasted, we returned in our coach to our lodgings."

The following day: "We all dined at that most obliging and universally curious Dr. Wilkins's at Wadham College. He was the first who showed me the transparent apiaries, which he had built like castles and palaces, and so ordered them one upon another, as to take the honey without destroying the bees. These were adorned with a variety of dials, little statues, vanes &c. . . . He also contrived a hollow statue, which gave a voice and uttered words by a long concealed pipe that went to its mouth, whilst one speaks through it at a good distance. He had, above in his lodgings and gallery, variety of shadows, dials, perspectives, and many other artificial, mathematical, and magical curiosities, a way-wiser, a thermometer, a monstrous magnet, conic and other sections, a balance on a demi-circle; most of them of his own, and that prodigious young scholar Mr. Christopher Wren; who presented me with a piece of white marble, which he had stained with a lively red, very deep, as beautiful as if had been natural. . . ."

Here we can taste the flavour of the active and varied pursuits from which, if at first the meanderings of dilettantism, emerged serious science. Ten years later, on October 24, 1664, Evelyn was again among the Oxford

"philosophers": "I went to visit Mr. Boyle (now here),
whom I found with Dr. Wallis and Dr. Christopher Wren,
in the tower of the schools, with an inverted tube, or
telescope, observing the discus of the sun for the passing
of Mercury that day before it. . . . so we went to see the
rarities in the Library, where the keepers showed me my
name among the benefactors. They have a cabinet of
some medals, and pictures of the muscular parts of man's
body. . . ."

It was not, however, all work for the senior and junior
members. A glance at Wood will provide a catalogue of
amusements, such as angling, swordsmanship, bell ringing, billiards, "birding," boating, bowls, cards, chess,
Christmas sports, cockfighting, dancing, fives, football,
fox hunting, horse racing, Maypoles, morris dancing, nut-
ting, rackets, running, skittles, tennis, walking, window
breaking, and wrestling, which show variety enough. Besides these diversions there were always entanglements
with women, and many were the cautions against bawdy-
houses. Several fellows, who until the last part of the nineteenth century were forced to remain celibate if they
did not wish to lose their fellowships, had bastard children left at their doors. Even if they were guiltless, in
many instances their reputation was seemingly not so high.

We hear much of laxity of discipline among undergraduates and their impositions, of which James Miller,
in his *Humours of Oxford* (1730), was to poke fun nearly
thirty years after Locke's death: "We have a company of
formal old surly Fellows who take pleasure in making one
act contrary to ones Conscience—and tho', for their own
parts, they never see the Inside of a Chappel throughout

the Year, yet if one of us miss but two mornings in a Week, they'll set one a plaguy *Greek* Imposition to do—that ne'er a one of them can read when tis done. And so i'gad I write it in *French*, for they don't know one from t'other."

The fact is that Oxford, not so far as all that from London, was really very isolated, and this isolation was due to the state of roads and to the fewness and discomfort of coaches and other forms of transport. For example, about 1670 the *Flying Coach* (according to William Hone's *Year-book*) took thirteen hours in summer to go from London to Oxford, while in winter it took two days. In 1707 there was only one carrier once a fortnight between Oxford and Bath, Oxford and Birmingham, and Oxford and Reading. To Shrewsbury there was one a month; to Exeter, one in five weeks; to Westmorland, three a year. On August 16, 1710, when Z. C. von Uffenbach, a German visitor, was driving from Bicester to Oxford, one of the wheels of the coach broke, and the passengers had to walk the remaining ten miles.

No wonder then that in this forced isolation spirits would out among the large section of youth, of both Town and Gown, and in Wood there are incidents like this during a mayoral election in September, 1673: "A scholar of Brase Nose his arm broke, another his head; began by servitors, and carried on by them, and commoners, and townsmen of the meaner sort." Such incidents are all the more understandable when one considers how the servitors—that is, poor scholars who had to work their way through the University by running errands for the more fortunate and serving in hall at meals—had to live. There is, for instance, an account of one of them who had to study "by the light of the rush candle on the staircase, with his feet in straw, not being able to afford fire and candle."

This brings us to Town as opposed to Gown. How did Town live in the days of Locke? It would be a good idea to look at the official City of Oxford during the period. As Sir John Marriott wrote: "The seventeenth century is perhaps the period in which Oxford stood nearest to the heart of national affairs. For nearly four years it was the capital of Royalist England, the home of the Court, the centre of administration, and the strategical head-quarters of the Cavaliers. Apart from the years of the Civil War, Oxford served throughout the century as a relief capital to London, when sickness raged in the latter city, or when the Stuart kings were anxious to try the effect of an enervating climate upon hot-headed politicians." This description, however, refers primarily to the University; the citizens who had come into their own during the Commonwealth looked with regret at least on the revival of episcopal and academic power. After 1660 there were many clashes between City and University.

If one glances through the Council Acts of the City of Oxford, one is able to reconstruct the official life of the City and its relationship with the University and a wider world. The first entry of note belongs to 1666 and reveals the University in an unfavourable light. In that year Dr. Wall, Canon of Christ Church, who had already given a thousand pounds to the City for charitable purposes, presented another thousand for the maintenance of thirty poor widows. When he died later in the year, only three members of his college attended his funeral, so angry were

41

the rest that he had left all his money to City and not to University charities.

In the same year there was a storm over the University's insistence on being in charge of the City market, an academic privilege jealously guarded since 1355, and a problem not solved till the end of the nineteenth century. Turning over further pages for this year, one is interested to come across the mention of three of the trade guilds of Oxford, the Cordwainers, the combined Smiths and Watchmakers, and the Tailors. Soon after this we come to the act which disallows the use of thatch on any houses in the City because of the danger of fire. Then there is a disagreement between the City and Merton College about Holywell Mill. Then comes an account of wages paid to the trumpeters and constables at the proclamation of the Treaty of Breda (1667), by which New Amsterdam (New York) was ceded by the United Provinces to England.

After a great quarrel between City and University, during which books and manuscripts were sent to London in support of either side, differences were patched up in time for the expensive entertainments the following year for the Lord Lieutenant and Deputy Lieutenants of the County.

We move on to 1670, when, just before Christmas, the Prince of Orange visited Oxford, while to 1672 belong the controversy about the boundary stones between the different parishes and the making of plans for repairing the Guildhall, which was carried out the next year. Differences between City and University about their respective rights to license citizens in various trades marked the year 1675, ending with the compromise by which, although the University kept its right of granting privileges to those skilled craftsmen whom it employed, a right it had held since the fourteenth century, the City held fast to its power of granting its freemen the right to pursue their trades without reference to the University.

The main happening of the year 1677–78 was the visit of the City's High Steward, the Duke of Buckingham, to Oxford, which was graphically described in the minutes of the Council. The City could do as well as the University when it came to such ceremonies:

"Upon his Grace's comeing to Oxon which was on Fryday the 2nd of November [1677] there was twenty gents of the Councell Chamber well mounted and Apparelled who by the command of Mr. Mayor and the Aldermen Attended his Grace's comeing att the end of our Franchises and Conducted him into the Citty Rideing in Comely manner two and two before his Grace's Coach, and upon his Grace's approach neare the Citty the Bells att St. Giles att Magdalene parish att St. Michaell's and St. Martin's did all Ring for Joy as he passed by but being Come to Pennylesse Bench the Citty Waites being placed upon the Leads there proclaymed his welcome and there Mr. Mayor and the Aldermen in their Scarlet Gownes, Cloakes and Tippets and the thirteene and Bayliffs in their Scarlett Gownes the Townclerke with a Gold Chayne and the Rest of the Councell in their Gownes in Decent manner being Accompanyed with severall other persons of Quality stood Ready to Receave his Grace, who was pleased to Alight out of his Coach and came to the Bench to them being Accompanyed with my Lord Lovelace and divers other persons of Honour. . . ."

After various speeches of welcome the Duke, that old libertine, of whom Alexander Pope in his epistle to Lord Bathurst, "Of the Use of Riches," was later to write:

"Gallant and gay, in Cliveden's proud alcove,
The bower of wanton Shrewsbury and love;
Or just as gay, at council, in a ring
Of mimick'd statesmen, and their merry King . . ."

"was pleased to Express his kinde Acceptance . . . of his Recepcon heere, And went Immediately with Mr Mayor and the Company through the Halls into the Councell Chamber from whence after some small stay there he went with Mr. Mayor and the Company to Mr Langstone's howse which was provided for his Recepcon, Where was a verry large table Covered with damask togeather with foote Cloathes and A Fayre Chaire for his Grace to sett to dinner, which table being Richly furnished with all manner of Costly provision Fish and Flesh."

After an enormous banquet, "his Grace haveing washed in a verry large Silver Bason with sweet water prepared for that purpose he was pleased to Sitt and discourse with the Company and to make many Expressions of his great satisfaction with his Entertaynement and to drinke some bottles of Wine with great Mirthe and freedome untill about Seaven AClock att night about which time with many kind Expressions of thanks to Mr. Mayor and the Citty tooke his Leave."

In January, 1679, the Cavalier Parliament, which had been in office for nearly eighteen years, ended, and the

Whigs were swept into power. Although Charles II soon dissolved the Parliament, precautions were taken so that anti-Court feeling should not spread, and troops were sent to Oxford. The City was Whig, the University Tory; and, although the notorious Titus Oates was refused a degree by the University, the City granted him his freedom and a bailiff's place.

Meanwhile, the new mayor, Robert Pawling, defied the University at many points, and, as Anthony à Wood tells us, "Whereas all Mayors in memorie of man used to be mealie mouthed and fearfull of executing their office for feare of loosing trade, this person is not, but walks in the nights to take townsmen in tipling houses, prohibits coffee to be sold on Sunday." Not content with usurping the University's privileges, Pawling was continually advising parents not to send their sons to the University, it being in his opinion such a debauched place.

The year 1680 was a no less disturbed year in Oxford than it was in England generally, and mobs became so unruly that the Mayor's bodyguard was increased, and the City Council was very careful about the amount of drink allowed on public occasions. Again the City showed its Whig and antipapist feelings, strongly approving of Lord Lovelace when he publicly drank a health "to the confusion of all Popish princes," referring to James, Duke of York. When later the same year the Duke of Monmouth was given the freedom of Oxford, the University, true to its Tory character, ignored him.

As we read on, a regular kaleidoscope of changing scenes comes before us. We see the Vice-Chancellor refusing to receive the Mayor and Corporation in St. Mary's

Church on St. Scholastica's Day because some members of the Council refused to attend "out of contempt" for the University. We see the street fights between Town and Gown, the drinking orgies in the Guildhall, and swarms of pedlars in the streets selling "glasses, knives and forks and other wares." The year 1681 was a time of fear, and when Stephen Colledge of Oxford, a supporter of Shaftesbury's party, was convicted of high treason, there were ugly scenes in the streets while apprentices demonstrated in his favour. For the next eighteen months the City struggled with the Crown over its privileges, but finally Charles II won, and the City Charter was surrendered. For the moment the City accepted the inevitable and went so far as to celebrate Thanksgiving Day for the "deliverance of His Majesty from the Rye House Plot" with bonfires and "an entertainment of wind musick, a barrel of ale and a fier" at Penniless Bench near Carfax in the middle of the City, while youths marched through the streets with cudgels, crying for the King and the Duke of York.

It is indeed a full-blooded and crude age. Now the City conduit runs with claret, girls "strewing herbs" along the way of processions, while the crowds cry, "Vivat Rex!" Now we see a criminal going to his death with a paper stating his crime pinned to him. We see bodies of the hanged being given to surgeons for dissection, the burning of the Pope in effigy. We see linkboys lighting a rich citizen home and charwomen going out haymaking, with background sounds of the beating of drums, trumpet calls, the firing of salutes, street vendors' cries, the noise from open-air markets. From Wood's pages we hear the elements lend their aid to the noise with the rattling of hail, the pattering of rain, and the pealing of thunder. Gales sometimes sweep through the City, and many are the "languid seasons" when "low fevers" creep into Oxford under cover of thick river mists.

The next few years see the death of Charles II and the short, troubled reign of his brother, James II, whose coronation the Mayor and Aldermen attend. Obadiah Walker, the Roman Catholic Master of University College, now comes into the picture with a request that the City sell him a piece of waste land on which to build a hospital "for sicke and sore persons." Long afterward, in 1700, his intention was carried out. A hospital was built (it still exists) in the Parish of St. Clement's beyond Magdalen Bridge with money bequeathed by William Stone, Principal of New Inn Hall, who had died fifteen years previously.

Much more prosaic is the account of the trouble the City had with butchers, a close and rich corporation, which, as we learn from H. E. Salter's *Properties of the City of Oxford*, was in the seventeenth century limited to twenty members, so that when an Oxford butcher died or retired, all below him moved up one place and a new butcher started in the twentieth shop. Presuming on their power and privileges, they sold their meat whenever and wherever they wanted without regard to byelaws, and it took some time to tame them, which was eventually done in the autumn of 1685.

That same autumn, in an atmosphere of the Court's suspicion of the City, troops were quartered on Oxford—we see the troopers pacing up and down the lower hall of the Town Hall silhouetted against the great log fire for

47

which the City had to pay—while, as Wood writes, "the proctors walk not because of the troopers for fear of being affronted by them." James II pays an official visit, and the Mayor and Aldermen take the opportunity of ingratiating themselves with him.

In the next eighteen months, however, all the royal interference with the City Charter which they brought caused a revulsion of feeling against the King. In September, 1688, the City's charter was surrendered, and when a new one was produced and read in public, "no ceremony [was] observed nor joy used on this occasion." But James II's reign was soon to be drawn abruptly to a close, and, the old charter being restored, all those City officers who had been removed by James were reinstated. Early in November, William of Orange landed at Torbay in Devon, and six weeks later James II fled to France. The general state of unrest in the City necessitated a day and a night guard.

During the interregnum, as if to still the doubts and fears of the citizens, Princess Anne (later Queen Anne) and her husband, Prince George of Denmark, visited Oxford. The Princess entered the City accompanied by the Earl of Northampton "with 500 horse leading the van." It must have been a stirring sight. "Her Royal Highness was preceded by the Bishop of London, at the head of a noble troop of gentlemen, his lordship riding in a purple cloak, martial habit, pistols before him, and his sword drawn, and his cornett [junior cavalry officer] had the inscription in golden letters on his standard *Nolumus leges Angliae mutari*." The Vice-Chancellor of the University and the doctors attended in their scarlet robes and made her a speech in English, and Prince George "received her royal highness at Christ Church quadrangle with all possible demonstrations of love and affection."

The year 1689 brought the end of uncertainty to the waiting city. William and Mary were proclaimed joint monarchs of England, and the populace enjoyed a liberal supply of wine and beer to celebrate the occasion. Before the proclamation William III had set all minds at rest with a letter to the Earl of Abingdon, the Lord High Steward, which is thus recorded in the City Minutes: "My Lord, . . . I desire you to remember me very kindly to Mister Mayor, the magistrates, and the whole City of Oxford assuring them my favour and protection on all occasions, and that I will take care the first opportunity to see them. I am your affectionate freind, W. Henry Orange." Yet, however reassuring the new King might be to the Mayor, the latter was soon involved in troubles with the University, the guilds, and the apprentices, and on one occasion at least water was thrown over him.

In 1692 the City freemen successfully defended their right to be imprisoned for debt only in the old tower by the North Gate, Bocardo, and from the dry lines of the Council Minutes we can reconstruct a pathetic scene which must have been familiar to Oxonians: the dangling out from the window in this tower "looking up to Carfax" of a bag lowered for alms to the street below with the cry, "Pity the poor Bocardo birds!"

The next event of particular significance took place late in 1694 and was of a domestic kind. It concerned the City's water supply. It was proposed that a waterworks should be built, so that water could be brought from it "by pipes into all the principal streets and lanes of the City to the end that the Inhabitants thereof may at easy rates be furnished with river water in theire houses uppon all occasions and may be supplyed with a present remedy in case of any accidental calamatous fire."

Until that time the water supply had been brought from Hinksey, a village south of Oxford, through a magnificent conduit, which was built at Carfax in 1616 by Otho Nicholson and which remained there until 1787, when it was removed in the interests of traffic congestion to Nuneham Park, a country estate near Oxford, where it still is. Now in 1694 a "cisterne" was to be built on a parcel of waste ground near the North Gate at the north end of Cornmarket Street, while a water wheel and two floodgates were to be erected at Folly Bridge, at the southern approach to the City.

The cistern was to be set up "in handsome, artificiall and workmanlike manner," and must be "artificially and ornamentally erected upon collumns or pillars of the heighte of ten foote from the pavement to the end that by the erecting thereof the market place may not be obstructed or narrowed, nor the inhabitants there any waies or prejudiced or hurt by the same and that the said Wheele or Engine and floodgate shall be soe artificially contrived and set up that thereby neither the navigation shall be any waies hindred nor the adjoining meadows any waies prejudiced by overflowing or otherwise."

Thus Folly Bridge became the headquarters of the water supply of Oxford, and the tower on it, known as Friar Bacon's Study, following the shadowy tradition that it had once been inhabited by the famous mediaeval scholar and scientist Roger Bacon, was perhaps fittingly used as its control tower from 1715 onwards.

In the Council Acts of 1695 we see the place where the old City almsmen sat at Carfax, Penniless Bench, and watch them going to church in their gowns on Sundays or "receiving treats civilly" on thanksgiving days. Late in the year William III paid a visit to Oxford. According to the City Minutes elaborate plans were made, but this account must be supplemented with the vivid one given by Anthony à Wood, which brings out the suspicious and cold side of the King's character, something which struck nearly everyone who came into contact with him. The University had provided a sumptuous banquet for him, but William refused to eat a morsel, "and a rabble of townsmen got in and seyzed upon the banquet in the face of the whole Universitie."

The year 1696 was one of factiousness in City politics with rivals to the Mayor's party sending ruffians with blackened faces to threaten and insult him and fight with his constables. The same year came the unveiling of the Assassination Plot, a Jacobite scheme to coincide with a French invasion of England, aimed at nothing less than the murder of William III. The City, lukewarm towards the King until then, warmed to him in common with the country at large, and a loyal address was sent to Kensington Palace. We can hear the cheers running through the market stalls, the cries of the old applewoman from whom Wood bought his fruit and gained some of his gossip in Merton Street "over against Beam Hall," until the fer-

vour reached the fishmongers standing under the Guildhall.

We leave the City early in September, 1697. The Treaty
of Ryswick, so important for England, since by it Louis
XIV of France was forced to give up James II's cause and
acknowledge William III as lawful King, has been signed.
Reports of this have just been brought to Oxford on this
cheerful early autumn morning. The City fathers meet
at once, and "upon the happy news of a peace which our
Hon. High Steward has this day communicated to the
Mayor it is agreed that the Mayor and his brethren will
meet in their scarlet at the Bench [at Carfax near Penniless Bench] at six o'clock this evening and have a bonfire
with the bells ringing and the City music playing as is
usual on such a joyful occasion."

III

Oxford and the Outer World

Much has been said about incidents in English politics which affected Oxford, and the interplay and counterplay of City and Country on significant matters. "Everything in England," wrote Hartley Coleridge in his *Northern Worthies*, "takes the shape and tune of politics." This statement is particularly true of the Age of Locke. Oxford had passed with the nation through some of the most stirring times to be found in the whole of British history.

The Civil War has already been touched on and all the evils it brought on the University and City; but it should be remembered that it was the Cavaliers who damaged the academic life of the place. Wood testifies to the Court's bad and corrupting behaviour, and he was no lover of Puritans. He observes that, while during the war the students were "much debauched and became idle by their bearing arms and keeping company with rude soldiers," on the other hand, under the Commonwealth the University again became a place of religious and useful learning. Even Clarendon in his Royalist *History* was bound to conclude that "things were less bad under the Commonwealth than might have been expected." Tribute must certainly be paid to the strong man of the period, John Owen (1616–83), who was Vice-Chancellor from 1651 to 1659. Originally an Anglican, as a result of a hatred of Laud and all his High Church dictatorial ways, he left Oxford in 1637 and, having rejected Presbyterianism and "the straight-jacket of Geneva," became an Independent and Oliver Cromwell's chaplain.

Then let us turn for a moment to a highly important day for Oxford, that day in May, 1649, when Cromwell and Fairfax paid their state visit to the City. They lodged at All Souls, and "after reception," wrote Wood, "one of the new Fellows of All Souls College spake a speech to them which, though bad, yet good enough for soldiers." The generals dined in hall at Magdalen, where "they had good cheer and bad speeches. After dinner they played at Bowls in the College Green." On the following Sunday they heard two sermons at St. Mary's Church, where the preachers "though rank Presbyterians prayed hard, if not heartily, for the Army and their blessed proceedings."

Cromwell assured the University that the army chiefs "know no Commonwealth could flourish without Learning, and that they, whatsoever the world said to the contrary, meant to encourage it, and were so far from subtracting any of their means that they purposed to add more . . . ." On the death of the Earl of Pembroke in 1650, Oxford elected Cromwell Chancellor. It was a sensible move. The following year John Owen was intruded into the Deanery of Christ Church and was soon appointed Vice-Chancellor by Cromwell. While all around him were people eager to destroy traditions, Owen maintained sense and tolerance, going so far as to allow the use of the proscribed Anglican liturgy, which at the Restoration brought him the praise of Clarendon and the offer of high preferment if he would conform, but he, we are told, "preferred principles to place." Owen deserves well of the University, and during a potentially dangerous period when anarchists were busily advocating a break with tradition, he preserved the essentials of continuity with the past.

Even so, at the Restoration, Charles II was nowhere hailed with greater enthusiasm than at Oxford. Is this surprising? In ringing words to be found in Bliss's edition of the *Reliquiae Hernianae* the position of those who returned to their University, bitter from penurious exile, is well explained:

"They had been despoiled of their property, rejected from their livings and subjected to every injury and insult at the hands of a rabble who thought themselves reformers, but had no other aim than their own advancement and the plunder of those which had anything to lose. Can we wonder at the popularity with which Charles II ascended his father's throne, or be surprised that Hearne and those who thought with him still adhered in the following reign to the race of the Stuarts?"

Royalists were, as far as possible, reinstated in the academic posts they had held in the time of Charles I, and "all tokens of monarchy that were lately defaced or obscured" were restored. Edward Hyde, Earl of Clarendon, a true reactionary, growing more so with the years and finally an embarrassment to Charles II's court, became Chancellor of the University in 1660 and so remained until his political fall and banishment seven years later. At the Restoration, Clarendon was in his heyday. He was a power in the land. His belief was that Oxford and the Church of England must be harnessed to the Crown; Clarendon as Chancellor of England and Chancellor of Oxford was in an excellent position to bring this about. The Act of Uniformity of 1662 was one of the results of this deliberate policy. By it every clergyman and all who held university posts and taught in schools were obliged to swear publicly thus or forfeit their professional status:

"I A.B. do declare that it is not lawfull upon any pretence whatsoever to take Armes against the King and that I do abhorr that traiterous Position of taking Armes by His Authority against His Person or against those that are commissioned by him And that I will conforme to the Liturgy of the Church of England as it is now by Law established And I do declare that I do hold there lies no Obligacion upon me or on any other person from the Oath commonly called the Solemne League and Covenant to endeavour any change or alteration of Government either in Church or State And that the same was in it selfe an unlawfull Oath and imposed upon the Subjects of this Realme against the knowne Laws and Liberties of this Kingdome."

Although in 1689 all these obligations were removed

except for the declaration of conformity to the liturgy of the Church of England, they were all in force during Locke's Oxford years, and it was for contravening the political clauses that he was outlawed and deprived of his fellowship.

With the Restoration, Oxford regained the political importance it had had under Charles I. Charles II paid Oxford a week's ceremonial visit in the autumn of 1663 as a sign of his favour; but two years later, as a result of the plague in London, the City became what a generation before it had been during the Civil War, the headquarters of the government of England. Throughout the autumn and winter of 1665–66 the undergraduate at least would have had to make way for the Lords and Commons and those idle courtiers whose "very nasty and beastly ways" Anthony à Wood deplored. King Charles lodged in Christ Church, Queen Catherine of Braganza at Merton, and (an insult to her and to the University surely) in Merton also lodged the King's current mistress, Lady Castlemaine, who bore a royal bastard while in college. Parliament sat in the Convocation House and pandered to Royalist reaction by passing while in session there the cruel Five Mile Act directed against Nonconformists.

When the plague died away in the course of the winter and Court and Parliament returned to London, Charles II must have stored in his mind his success in overawing the Commons when it was isolated from the capital; and when later in his reign a crisis threatened, he determined to draw the claws of the Commons in Oxford. In 1680 the Commons had dared to pass the Exclusion Bill to prevent the succession to the Crown of James, Duke of York, who

57

was "notoriously known to have been perverted from the Protestant to the Popish Religion." The Lords rejected the bill, but the Commons persisted and refused to vote money to the King. Charles's answer was to dissolve Parliament and order a new one to meet at Oxford. Charles II knew his Oxford. He realised that the University was grateful to him for the privileges he had given it, and in that alien atmosphere, so different from crowded, critical, violent London, the Commons could easily be subdued.

Even so, many Whig members came defiantly to the University City armed and with armed escorts. The King compromised to the point of a regency under William of Orange, but the Whigs saw through this ruse; nothing but absolute exclusion of the papist Duke of York was enough for them. They had, however, overreached themselves, and the cunning King, taking advantage of his personal popularity, dissolved Parliament once more. Two glimpses of him, personally recorded by a visitor who in her old age in the following century used to relate them to her friends, belong to this time: the one on the anxious first day of the Oxford Parliament in March, 1681, when the tall, dark, frowning King, his robe flung carelessly over his arm, was seen striding across the quadrangle on his way to the Sheldonian Theatre to face his recalcitrant Commons; and later, when he had triumphed that same King Charles, relaxed and smiling, walking through the parks with his pet spaniels.

The University was proud that the Crown had sought refuge and gained a triumph in the City and in the summer of 1683 made the most of the horror evoked by the disclosure of the Rye House Plot to murder the King to pass a decree against "pernicious books and damnable doctrines," at the same time condemning as "false, seditious and impious" Hobbes's view that resistance to the Crown could in any circumstances be lawful. Although not all members of the University agreed with this view, the majority strongly supported the witch-hunt, and the Court took advantage of the situation to eject all Whig academics. In the following year Vice-Chancellor John Fell, much against his will, was forced to obey the royal mandate and remove the name of John Locke from Christ Church.

So strong, in fact, was the Royalist reaction during the last months of Charles II's life that at his death his brother James, for all his Catholicism, peacefully succeeded to the throne. Thus James II came in with the false hopes which a few years later were to ruin him. He had been greatly encouraged by the Decree of 1683 and by the University's loyalty to him during the Monmouth rebellion, and was now determined to make Oxford the starting point of his attack on the established Protestant Church. In his own words he had come to regard the University as "the magazine and arsenal of the Anglican Church." In capturing it he would be taking the first step in bringing England back to Rome.

Oxford was now, as so many times before, the mirror of England. Like the country at large it was torn between loyalty to the Crown and loyalty to the Church. James II resolved to fight his opponents to the death; his battle with Oxford was the preliminary to his fight with England, and from the start he threw all discretion and wisdom to the winds.

He started by issuing dispensations to Obadiah Walker, Master of University College, and two fellows to continue to hold their offices, although they were declared Roman Catholics, and in 1686 he followed up this action by granting a similar dispensation to Dr. Massey, Dean of Christ Church, a Catholic convert. A year later by his Declaration of Indulgence he made an end of all penal laws against Roman Catholics and Protestant Nonconformists, in fact in favour of all enemies of Anglicanism. He, however, failed to win over the Nonconformists, who saw that what James intended in the long run was the political enslavement of the country.

The epic of Magdalen College's resistance to the King began early in 1687 when Dr. Clerke, the President of the college, died and royal orders were sent to the fellows to elect in his place a Roman Catholic convert, Anthony Farmer, a man both immoral in character and academically unqualified according to the college statutes. The fellows thereupon refused to elect him and chose their own President, and when called before the Ecclesiastical Commission for contumacy proved their point about Farmer, but were ordered to elect another of the King's nominees. James II backed up this command by coming to Oxford himself and interviewed the fellows, but even this had not the desired effect; still they refused to obey and were all expelled. By this time the whole of England was watching; it was as it were the dress rehearsal for the resistance of the seven bishops in the following year. The point of view of the Oxford resisters was to be that of the nation a year later: devotion to Church came before devotion to Crown.

Here is Oxford in her dealings with the political world of England, and all the while culturally, scientifically, academically, as in the realms of faith the University was exerting a growing influence, not only on England but also on Europe.

During the seventeenth century Oxford University began to gather in the cultural treasures which partly compensated for what had been destroyed in the iconoclastic times of the Reformation. Much silver was lost in being melted down in the King's cause during the Civil War, but other prizes were to come Alma Mater's way.

Two generations before Locke went to Oxford the University's books and manuscripts had been worthily housed thanks to Sir Thomas Bodley, and in Locke's early graduate days the noble library was increased by the addition to it of the collection of the scholar and jurist John Selden (1584–1654), a wing of the old library being called to this day Selden End. This gift of books came to Oxford in 1659, and the following year Selden's collection of "antique marbles" was also transferred to the University. Indeed, Oxford like the many great virtuosos of the time was concerning itself with collecting not just volumes needed in the pursuit of learning, but objects of art as well. This was the age in which a scholar's study contained collections of coins and medals, Roman lamps and seals, a bust or two, Venetian glass, intaglios, and terra-cotta statuettes. The Grand Tour had already begun, noble travellers were abroad scouring Italy, and King Charles I had led the way by forming his magnificent collection of pictures and bestowing his patronage on Sir Anthony Van Dyck.

Such a lover of works of art was Thomas Howard, Earl of Arundel (1586–1646), only and posthumous son of the ill-fated Philip, Lord Arundel, who died in the Tower of London, a victim of Elizabeth I's persecution of the Roman Catholics. Thomas Howard flourished at the courts of James I and Charles I, holding many important posts and travelling abroad far and wide, especially in France and Italy. He soon became known as an outstanding collector. During the Civil War he left England and went to Italy, where John Evelyn met him in Padua in June, 1645. This passage is redolent with the flavour of the world of the Grand Tour and the virtuoso:

"This morning, the Earl of Arundel, now in this city, a famous collector of paintings and antiquities, invited me to go with him to see the garden of Mantua, where, as one enters, stands a huge colosse of Hercules. From thence to a place where was a room covered with a noble cupola, built purposely for music; the fillings up, or cove, betwixt the walls, were of urns and earthen pots, for the better sounding; it was also well painted. After dinner, we walked to the Palace of Foscari all'Arena, there remaining yet some appearances of an ancient theatre, though serving now for a court only before the house."

Oxford was to profit from the Earl's travels when, twenty-three years later, Evelyn persuaded his second son, who had succeeded to half of the fine Arundel collections, to present some important marbles, including the outstandingly interesting "Parian Chronicle," to the University. This was the nucleus of a varied museum which Oxford was soon to have, and a museum, as the Italian and Dutch universities had already shown, was a pre-

requisite of an academic institution and indeed comple-
mentary to a library. However, the Arundel collection
was very far from being enough to fill a museum. It was
Elias Ashmole (1617-92) —that strange mixture of cre-
dulity and knowledge, of sense and extravagance, medical
quack, astrologer, busying himself with the infinite details
of heraldry, collector of valuables and rubbish—who was
the father of Oxford's museum, which was called after
him; and when in the nineteenth century the new museum of fine arts and antiquities was opened in Beaumont
Street, that also bore his name. The first museum, now
called the Old Ashmolean and containing perhaps the
finest collection of old scientific instruments in the world,
is the one which concerns us here. It was completed in
1683, and the following year Ashmole's collections, aug-
mented by those of John Tradescant, Royal Gardener to
Charles I, and his son, were set out in the fine new building. It was to be not only "a collection of curiosities" but
a centre for science also, and was one of the triumphs of
seventeenth-century Oxford. Anthony à Wood has much
to say of it:

"*Musaeum Ashmoleanum, Oxon.* A large and stately
pile of stone squared, but at the charg of the Universitie,
who found such a building necessary in order to the pro-
moting and carrying on with greater ease and success
severall parts of usefull and curious learning, for which
it is so well contrived and designed.—It bordures upon
the west end of the Theater [the Sheldonian], having a
very magnificent portall on that side, sustained by pillars
of the Corinthian order with several curious frizes and
other artificial embellishments. The front (about 60

feet) is to the street northward, where is this inscription over the entrance in gold characters:—

MUSAEUM ASHMOLEANUM: SCHOLA NATURALIS HISTORIAE: OFFICINA CHIMICA

"The first foundation was laid 14 Apr. 1679 and it was happily finished on the 20 March 1682/3, at which time a rich and noble collection of curiosities was presented to the University by that excellent and public-spirited gentleman, Elias Ashmole, esq., a person so well knowne to the world that he needs no further *elogium* . . ., and the same day there deposited, and afterwards digested and put into a just series and order by the great care and diligence of the learned Robert Plot, LL.D., who at the worthy donor's request is entrusted with the custody of the Musaeum.—By the beginning of May following the rarities were all fixed in their distinct cabinets and places and the roome furnished in every part of it: but it was not opend publicly till after 21 day of that month, on which day their royall highnesses the duke and duchess of York and the princess Ann . . . were first entertain'd in it. . . . Take this brief description of this building:—It consists of 10 rooms, whereof the three principal and largest are public, being each in length about 56 feet and in breadth 25. The uppermost is properly the *Musaeum Ashmoleanum*, where an inferior officer alwaies attends to show the rarities to strangers.—The middle roome is the *School of Natural Historie*, where the professor of chymistry, who is at present Dr. Robert Plot, reads three times a week . . . concerning all natural bodies relating to and made use of in chymicall preparations, particularly as to the countries and places where they are produced and found, their natures, their qualities and virtues, their effects, by what marks and characteristicks they are distinguished one from another, natural from artificial, true from sophisticated, with their several mixtures and preparations in trials and experiments, with the entire process of that noble art, verie necessary to the cure of diseases when carefully managed by learned and skilfull persons. —The lower room, a cellar to which there is a descent by a double pair of staires, is the *Laboratory* perchance one of the most beautiful and useful in the world, furnished with all sorts of furnaces and all other necessary materials in order to use and practice, which part is with very great satisfaction performed by Mr. Christopher White, the skilfull and industrious operator of the University....

"Neare adjoining to the laboratory are two faire roomes, whereof one is designed for a *chymical librarie,* to which several books of that argument have been already presented.—The other is made use of as a *store roome for chymical preparations,* where such as stand in need of them are furnished at easie rates, the design of this building being not onlie to advance the studies of true and real philosophie but also to conduce to the uses of life and the improvement of medicine.—Neare the Musaeum [amended by Wood to 'under the same roof'] is a handsome roome fitted for a *Library of Natural History and Philosophy.*

"The other remaining chambers are the lodging chamber and studies of the Keeper of the Musaeum, whereof one which is most convenient is sometimes employed and made use of for private courses of anatomy.

"Accessions are continually made to the musaeum by several worthy persons, as Dr. Robert Huntingdon, who hath given hieroglyphicks and other Aegyptian antiquities; Mr. Aaron Goodyear, to whose generous favour they owe there an intire mummy; and the learned Martin Lister, Dr. of Phys., who has presented the University with a large cabinet of natural rarities of his owne collection and of sevarel Roman antiquities, as altars, medalls, lamps, etc. found here in England. So that it is justly believed that, in few yeares, it will be one of the most famous repositories in Europe."

It may here be noticed that this century saw a great revival of herbal medicine in England, in which Oxford took a foremost part. Already, following the lead of several continental universities, notably Leyden, as mentioned above, a Botanical or "Physic" Garden had been established opposite Magdalen College (where it still remains) by Henry, Earl of Danby, in 1632. Its first superintendent was the German horticulturalist Jakob Bobart, who in 1648 published his famous *Catalogue of Plants in the Garden*. After the Restoration, Robert Morison of Aberdeen took over the professorship of botany and gave the "Physic" Garden all his attention, ably summing up his life's work in his book *Plantarum historia universalis Oxoniensis* (1680). When the German traveller Uffenbach came to Oxford in 1710 and admired its buildings and gardens, it was to the younger Jakob Bobart, who succeeded Morison and added a second volume to his work, that he addressed himself.

Yes, plants for the health of the body as well as for the delight of the eye meant much to the world in an age so much more natural than ours; and to round off this side of the matter let John Evelyn speak to us again from Padua:

"The next morning I saw the garden of simples. rarely furnished with plants, and gave order to the gardener to make me a collection of them for an *hortus hyemalis* [winter garden], by permission of the Cavalier Dr. Veslingius [Johann Vesling, a German, 1598–1649], then Prefect and Botanic Professor as well as an Anatomy."

There was another great benefactor of Oxford in Locke's lifetime, Colonel Christopher Codrington, fellow of All Souls College, who died in 1693 after a successful career in the army and as an estate owner in Barbados, leaving the college his valuable library and ten thousand pounds for a building in which to house it. Although the building was not erected until the following century, this great law library was already in use before Locke died, and thanks to it legal studies had already been materially strengthened.

Many of the college buildings we see today date from this time. It was the age of that "debased Gothic" (a term which implies no disparagement of it) peculiar to Oxford, carried out by local masons working in Headington stone, so called from a quarry nearby. There are few Oxford colleges today which do not contain features in this style. It was the age also of Italianesque architecture, the florid Classic, ancient Rome seen through late Renaissance eyes. Let us take a survey of the buildings of the seventeenth century in Oxford. First the Sheldonian Theatre, which was built between 1664 and 1669 according to Wren's plans and the design of which was suggested by the Amphitheatre of Marcellus at Rome. Faithful to his supposed classical model and remembering that, of course, the original would have had no roof, the builders gave it a flat ceiling in imitation of a canvas covering over gilt cords stretched from side to side. The Old Ashmolean, another creation of the time, has already been described.

In the Convocation House and the Old Schools Quadrangle, in one angle of which is the Bodleian Library, one finds examples of seventeenth-century architects rebuilding in the perpendicular tradition but in the spirit of their own age. Thus while the general plan of both is mediaeval, conventual one might say, the external features are florid. The Convocation House, of a simpler and severer style, was completed in 1640. In the Old Schools Quadrangle, built in 1439 but basically altered in 1613–18, one sees the general architectural spirit prevailing in Oxford in Locke's time, and which is to be noticed in the rebuilding of the colleges undertaken in his day to preserve the general setting carried down from the Middle Ages while softening and embellishing it. The Old Schools Quadrangle was the hub of the University; here the faculties met, as the blue and gold inscriptions over the various doors indicate, and here until the opening of the New Examination Schools in the High Street in 1882 all examinations (all of them oral in Locke's day) were held. Standing in this quadrangle is the remarkable

Schools Tower, mediaeval in general character but orna-
mented with columns of the five orders of Classic architecture, grouped in pairs—Tuscan, Doric, Ionic, Corinthian, and Composite.

Of all the colleges Wadham, the first stone of which was
laid in 1610, is the finest and most characteristic group
of collegiate buildings of the seventeenth century. Particularly impressive are the elegant Chapel, which contains excellent glass by Bernard van Ling (1620), the
stone-vaulted gateway, and the Hall with its handsome
screen and high timber roof. Balancing the Chapel on
the other side of the Hall is the Library. The whole is a
striking example of debased Gothic, all of a piece and at
its best. The beautiful little quadrangle of St. Edmund
Hall, with its Chapel and Library dating from 1680, is
another triumph of the seventeenth century.

Queen's College began to lose its mediaeval character
in the 1690's, when the great programme of rebuilding
started. The Hall was probably designed by Nicholas
Hawksmoor, a pupil of Wren, but the Library, definitely
by Wren, has a fine ceiling and wood carvings by Grinling
Gibbons. The Chapel, however, is cold and heavy and is
the result, together with much else in the college, of the
second rebuilding period of 1710 in the Palladian style.
Queen's was regarded in the eighteenth century as the
"noblest" and most "refined" edifice in Oxford.

Brasenose College's Chapel of 1668 with an excellent
fan-tracery roof is just what Locke, Wood, and their contemporaries would have considered the last word in cor-
rect taste. Oriel College was completely rebuilt during
the 1630's and up to the outbreak of the Civil War, and

its jewel is the Caroline Hall with its charming entrance portico, approached by a flight of steps and surmounted by a curious parapet. Its oak roof is the most beautiful of its period in the country.

St. John's College shows a happy blending of the mediaeval and the seventeenth century in the front quadrangle, while the second quadrangle is a triumph of the earlier Stuart period. It was completed in 1636 under the eye of Archbishop Laud, then Chancellor of the University and President of the College. The effect of the colonnades, or piazzas, in the Italianesque manner, probably designed by no less an architect than Inigo Jones, architect of the Banqueting Hall of Whitehall, London, is very striking. The long battlemented Library looking out over the garden belongs to the same period.

Trinity College with its wider quadrangles, divided up into groups of buildings with avenues, groves, and gardens, shows the seventeenth century breaking away from the formal, conventual idea. The Chapel was designed in 1694 by an amateur architect, the college's own President Bathurst, and its screen and altarpiece are of beautifully carved cedarwood, as at Queen's by England's greatest wood carver, Grinling Gibbons, Locke's contemporary. The scent of the exotic wood still breathes over the cool marble. The Hall was only about fifty years old in Locke's day, a tasteful Jacobean building which could fitly stand in a well-bred parkland, and the illusion which Trinity gives of being a great private mansion is increased by the fine East Gate, which leaves one with the impression of the entrance to a stately home; the concept of conventualism has vanished, for the college has become not the home of the hard-working young gownsman, but the residence of young lords and gentlemen. Wren was busy designing the third quadrangle in Locke's day, and by 1682 it was completed.

Exeter College Hall is another example of the debased Gothic peculiar to Oxford, as is practically the whole of Jesus College, except for the north side, which is modern. Its first quadrangle was finished in 1636, the Hall a little later, and the Library in 1667.

Finally in the list of buildings which were erected in Locke's century comes Lincoln College Chapel, completed in 1642, one of the most interesting examples of seventeenth-century work in Oxford. It was built on a mediaeval plan and was fitted up with cedar and oak in Renaissance style. The Flemish glass in the windows, brought from Italy in 1629, is particularly choice.

These are the buildings which Locke's Oxford has bequeathed to us; remove the seventeenth-century architecture and you leave an enormous gap impossible to fill. In fact at this period the losses caused by the devastations of the Reformation were in part at least made good.

After the Restoration, Oxford in common with London began to pick up its Continental threads; like its King it tended—at least tended—towards France, and Oxonians were eager that the University of Paris should learn of its physical beauties. Archbishop Laud had already shown that Oxford could concern itself with theological and other scholarly matters which brought it into direct contact with leaders of the Greek Orthodox Church. Laud had already attempted to reconcile the Anglican and Orthodox churches and had even engaged in amicable controversy with the Jesuits. In Locke's time George Bull of Exeter College, Oxford, afterwards Bishop of St. David's, published his *Judicium Ecclesiae Catholicae* (1694), which went a long way towards bringing about a friendly relationship with the French Gallican Church and especially with the famous Bishop Jacques Bossuet. This is an example of how Oxford was already making intellectual contact with the outer world; but it was displaying its physical wares as well.

Until the Reformation, Oxford had been glad to share with the rest of Europe in the heritage of knowledge; but thereafter she became complacent. The poor scholars were at a discount; she became part of the Establishment. The trials and tribulations of civil war, and then the return of a royal court, most of the members of which from Charles II downwards had spent the Commonwealth years in France or Spain or Italy, were reflected in Oxford's attitude after 1660. The University with its newly regained importance as one of the great centres of learning in Europe wanted to be admired distantly. She disliked the idea of foreign scholars seeking her out and perhaps trying to foist new ideas on her, and for a very long time she gave all Continental visitors a chilly welcome; but that did not mean that she was not ready to show herself off to those who lived far away and might spread her renown to the far corners of Europe. Above all, the University of Paris, ever a rival and the intellectual eye of France, now a political menace to England, might be humbled by seeing, at least in the form of engravings, the architectural beauties of her colleges and public buildings. What would the paltry college buildings of Paris University—the Dix-Huit, the Harcourt, the Sorbonne and all the others—amount to if set beside magnificent copperplate renderings of Magdalen, Merton, and Christ Church?

This idea led to the creation of that beautiful and much-prized volume, *Oxonia Illustrata* (1675). It was John Fell (1625–86), Dean of Christ Church, who conceived the idea for such a book, and he found just the man to execute the engravings in David Loggan (1635?–1700), a native of Danzig, who settled in England shortly before the Restoration. In his hands exquisite bird's-eye views of all the University buildings came into being, not just isolated architectural records, but a living pictorial account of the Oxford of the day (practically all of it still existing), with academic figures in cap and gown meeting in the quadrangles, servants rolling barrels to the cellars, gardeners at work elsewhere, while outside a college gate a hay wain passes, or a carriage-and-four, here and there a citizen on horseback, and a husbandman coming from the fields, spade over shoulder. Comfortable plumes of sea-coal smoke belly out from the chimney stacks. It is workaday Oxford in the reign of Charles II, and what an Oxford! One in which a scholar sitting in his study can look out across the fields and see the gathering of the harvest.

The book that delights us had its effect. The University of Paris took note and published its own topographical prints, which if you study them in the Bibliothèque Nationale only go to show how poor were its buildings, to say nothing of the inferior craftsmanship of the engravers.

Beautiful, however, as Oxford's buildings appear in *Oxonia Illustrata*, they would indeed be hollow if they lacked men worthy to live and work in them; but in Locke's time such were not wanting. Much has already been mentioned about this intellectual golden age. Here are names to light up a galaxy of varied genius, many of whom Locke knew and lived among:

Henry Aldrich (1647–1710), logician, whose *Artis Logicae Compendium* remained a standard textbook for a century, architect, who designed the Peckwater Quadrangle at Christ Church, Trinity College Chapel, and the Church of All Saints, and musicologist and composer; Richard Allestry (1619–81), a great theologian and Provost of Eton; Elias Ashmole (1617–92), scientist and antiquarian, whose name, as we have seen, is commemorated in the Ashmolean Museum; John Aubrey (1626–97), antiquary and topographer, one of those delightful eccentrics in which Oxford has always abounded; and Edward Hyde, Earl of Clarendon (1608–74), whose connection with Oxford rose from that of undergraduate of Magdalen Hall to Chancellor of the University and who, apart from his political career, which lives as English history, wrote his majestic *History of the Rebellion*.

Next may be cited Nathaniel Crewe (1633–1722), Bishop first of Oxford and then of Durham, who took a leading part in the politicoreligious turmoils of the reign of James II and the "Glorious Revolution," and whose benefaction heads of colleges and doctors of the University of Oxford still enjoy before walking in procession to the Sheldonian Theatre at Encaenia (or Commemoration) each year; and after him that man of much more noble character Henry Dodwell (1641–1711), the learned classical historian and geographer, the author of *An Account of the Ancient Geographers* and *Dissertations on the Ages of Phalaris and Pythagoras.*

Then there were Edmund Halley (1656–1742), the great astronomer, whose handsome house still stands in New College Lane, and Robert Hooke (1635–1703), who, although not a matriculated member of the University, received an honorary degree from it in 1663 and spent some years in the City in experimental research, being a founder fellow of the Royal Society. Then might be mentioned Thomas Hyde (1636–1703), astronomer and Arabic and Hebrew scholar; Sir Leoline Jenkins (1623–85), diplomat and benefactor of the University; Gerard Langbaine the Younger (1656–92), who held the official University post of Esquire Beadle of Law and is still famed for his *Account of the English Dramatic Poets;* Robert Plot (1640–96), the naturalist, whose weather diary is one of the first of its kind and the most valuable; and Edward Pococke (1604–91), one of the greatest Oriental scholars who ever lived.

Humphrey Prideaux (1648–1724), whose *Marmora Oxoniensia* (1676) marked a stage in the history of the criticism of monumental art, should have his place here, as also John Wallis (1616–1703), great mathematician, archivist, and generally considered to be the first practitioner of the deaf-and-dumb language; Seth Ward (1617–89), yet another astronomer and later Bishop of Salisbury; John Wilkins (1614–72), who may be termed the father of the Royal Society, since while Warden of Wadham College during the Civil War he formed the "Philosophical Association," which, after the Restoration, became the Royal Society. And then what of Christopher Wren (1632–1723), architect without peer, who from 1661 to 1673 was a leading light in Oxford?

In Locke's day so great was the activity at Oxford in the cause of the new science that this matter must have a chapter to itself, but it is more than necessary to point out here that Oxford scholars of those times were not mere scientists but had been classically educated, were interested in the fine arts, could take their part in philosophical controversy, and were in fact still all-round men in the fine Renaissance tradition. They certainly gave its stamp to the Royal Society, which down to the nineteenth century still had fellows' places for the learned who were not mere scientists; but we "know more and more about less and less," and today the Royal Society admits only certain kinds of scientists.

To illustrate the amazing advance in nonscientific studies in seventeenth-century Oxford, lest the chapter on science in the University which follows may seem to eclipse them, a glance at the development of Egyptology there would be worthwhile.

The seventeenth century saw an increasing number of scholars travelling to Egypt, and Oxford men were at the forefront. Outstanding among them was John Greaves (1602–52), professor of astronomy at Oxford, author of *Pyramidographia* (1646), the first important English work on Egyptology. He studied the pyramids at first hand, making a remarkable drawing of a section of the Great Pyramid of Giza, and brought back with him Egyptian manuscripts and various "curiosities." In 1636, Archbishop Laud may be said to have become the father of the subject at Oxford when he presented valuable Egyptian manuscripts and ceramics and a finely cut, hieroglyphically inscribed coffin lid to the Bodleian Library. Then in 1683, the year of the opening of the Ashmolean Museum, Robert Huntingdon (1637–1701), fellow of Merton and chaplain to the Levant Company from 1670 to 1681, made many splendid gifts of Egyptian antiquities to the University, including what is still the best piece of Old Kingdom relief sculpture in Oxford (Fourth Dynasty, circa 2600 B.C.), a cornice for a false door in the mastaba at Saqqara of a high official called Sheri. Even though it was to be long before Champollion appeared to read the hieroglyphics, the raw material was already to hand in Oxford, thanks to the eager search after knowledge by indomitable scholars travelling far and wide in an alien and dangerous Mohammedan world.

IV

Oxford and Science

The seventeenth century, that period of growing scientific interest, affected Oxford but gradually at first. Francis Bacon had led the way along the lines that experimentation is the only means by which physical problems can be investigated. As the famous visit of John Milton to Italy illustrates, the Grand Tour, emanating from Renaissance culture, now widespread in England as elsewhere, introduced many to the climate of the new scientific ideas at that very moment richly flowering in Italy. There were many "Tuscan artists" to be found looking through their "optick glasses"

> "At evening from the top of Fesolé,
> Or in Valdarno, to descry new lands . . ."

on the moon. Travellers to Italy returned with new ideas, having overheard and overseen the new knowledge.

One of these travellers was Sir Henry Wotton, who in 1584 had matriculated at New College. Until his death in 1639, aged over seventy, he retained a lively interest in science, a dabbler perhaps, but one of those questioning souls who opened side doors on the physical world, through which men might come and go until the larger ones were cut. He made the Grand Tour and profited from it; yet it was not in Italy but in Austria that he witnessed the new science in action, for it was in the house of the great Johannes Kepler at Linz that he saw experiments being carried out, an account of which he communicated to Bacon himself in 1620. Wotton did some useful work on water clocks, a subject which had all down the years hardly advanced beyond the simple Roman clepsydra, and was a patient investigator of methods of distillation of fruit, herbs, and vegetables for medicinal purposes. Distillation was the primary interest of John French of New Inn Hall, who died in 1657 as a physician to the English army in France.

Since the middle of the sixteenth century nearly every Italian town had been able to boast an academy, sometimes for the arts or the sciences and sometimes for both together. The idea of forming one in London for science on a similar model was made by Theodore Haak, "a German of the Palatinate." Meetings were held from 1645 in private houses, in taverns, and sometimes at Gresham College, that institution founded in the interests of higher learning in London by the munificent Sir Thomas

Gresham during the reign of Elizabeth I, and the topics seem to have been particularly directed to astronomy.

The growing difficulties which London was experiencing as a result of the Civil War ended the learned meetings there, but Oxford benefited. Here in 1649 came many who had attended these London meetings, and for some time the University City was the centre of English science. Every week an "experimentall philosophicall clubbe" was held, and amongst the group to be found there regularly were such famous names in Oxford scientific history as Thomas Willis, William Petty, Ralph Bathurst, and Seth Ward. The place of meeting was first at Petty's rooms at Brasenose, then at the lodgings of John Wilkins, Warden of Wadham (and later Bishop of Chester), who had been one of the original London members, and then from 1654 "at the lodgings of the Honourable Mr. Robert Boyle."

We have now come to the name of a great scientist connected with Oxford, Robert Boyle, although he was not a member of the University. Boyle, one of the many sons of the Earl of Orrery, had come from his native Ireland in disgust at the state of science there, and on the advice of his old friend and mentor Dr. (afterwards Sir) William Petty (1623–87), the anatomist and inventor of a copying machine, or pentagraph, and further encouraged by the invitation of Warden Wilkins, he settled in Oxford. Young though he was, he had already made scientific history by being the first to prepare hydrogen and to explain the distinction between chemical compounds and mixtures. This gifted but prim and cold young man (he was already a notorious vivisector) worked by the light of his own dictum: "Experiment is the interrogation of Nature."

In the summer of 1654 he accordingly began to reside in a house in High Street on the west side of University College, remaining there until 1668. (The building stood until 1809, when with adjoining property it was demolished, the greater part of the site being eventually occupied by Barry's new University College buildings and the Shelley Memorial. A plaque commemorating Boyle's occupancy of the original building has recently been put up on the wall of the Memorial facing the street.) As one can imagine, Boyle's lodgings soon became the Mecca of Oxford scientists.

On July 13, as mentioned above, in the year Boyle arrived in Oxford, John Evelyn recorded in his diary his visit to Warden Wilkins, particularly interesting because Wilkins probably owned the finest collection of scientific instruments in England. He insisted on proper laboratories, and Boyle was to profit from Wilkins' declaration that simple, portable instruments which could be set up in any ordinary living room were not satisfactory for serious experimentation. Wilkins was indeed "universally curious"—the glass-covered apiary which he gave to Evelyn was later "contemplated" by Charles II "with much satisfaction"—and owned thermometers, conic sections, balances, a telescope, magnets, dials, "shadows," and a "rare burning glasse." Boyle, working on these foundations, gradually built up a finely equipped laboratory, the archetype of all such for the future.

Francis Bacon had half a century earlier proposed that there should be a national research laboratory, others in the meantime had echoed the wish for such an institution, and now something of the kind was growing up in the

Oxford of the Commonwealth. By 1659, according to Anthony à Wood, the interest in chemistry was spreading throughout the University. Wood wrote, retrospectively (the actual Royal Society of London not being founded till 1662):

"The Royal Society at Oxon did, in Clerk's house, an apothecary in St. Marie's parish, exercise themselves in some chimicall extracts, which were carried on and much improved before the king's restauration, in so much that severall Scholars had privat elaboratories and did performe those things which the memory of man could not reach."

We also gather from Wood that public lectures on chemistry began about this time.

Boyle's laboratory was no doubt the pivot of all this activity, and in the years after the Restoration its reputation spread to London, for the important communications placed by Boyle before the Royal Society, now established there, were the results of his unwearied activities in the High Street laboratory. His chief assistant was Robert Hooke (1635–1703), who played a great part in building the famous air pump in 1660 and who was later to become a scientist in his own right. That same year Boyle's "pneumatic engine," as it was also called, was acclaimed in Paris.

In 1661 was published in Oxford that great classic of chemistry, Boyle's *The Sceptical Chymist*, in which among other things he defined an "element," made a plea for experiment in place of abstract reasoning, and described his discoveries of how to produce methyl alcohol and acetone. His other book published at Oxford was *Experi-*

ment on Colours (1663) , in which he described the action of acids and alkalis and the use of various vegetable dyes. Meanwhile he was busy with chemical and physiological experiments and kept up a lively interest in astronomy and meteorology. Before he left for London in 1668, he had probably begun his experiments on metals, especially tin, iron, lead, and copper, which are said to have provided the basis for Antoine Lavoisier's experiments in the latter part of the eighteenth century. It may here be noted that Boyle, however, mistakenly attributed the gain in weight to the absorption of ponderable heat which gave rise to the ludicrous "phlogiston" theory. Given such a cue by Boyle and others such as Becher, Georg Ernst Stahl of Halle set out on that wrong path which was to lead chemistry astray for the best part of a century.

As early as 1659 chemistry classes were being held in the University, and the lecturer had been brought over by Boyle. He was Peter "Sthael" (probably Stahl, but not related to G. E. Stahl) called by Wood "the noted chimist and Rosicrucian, . . . of Strasburgh in Royal Prussia, a Lutheran, a great hater of women, and a very useful man." Records of his classes and those who attended them have been preserved for us by the indefatigable Wood, the most important of Sthael's followers being John Wallis, Professor of Geometry; Christopher Wren; and John Locke himself. Of Locke, Wood has preserved this malicious thumbnail picture, rather the result of gossip gleaned at second hand (for Wood never knew him) from jealous enemies than anything approximating reality:

"A man of turbulent spirit, clamorous and never contented. The Club wrote and took notes from the mouth of their master, who sat at the upper end of a table; but the said J. Lock scorned to do it; so that while every man besides of the club were writing, he would be prating and troublesome."

All the same, as some letters of his prove, Locke was enthusiastic enough in 1666 to carry out in Christ Church some experiments in distillation. It is amusing to imagine the philosopher (as Locke himself describes it) "not being fully acquainted with the way Helmont [J. B. van Helmont, the chemist] mentions he made use of to preserve juices," opening his flower juices, when, "though when I took off the head from the body [of the retort], it had been several hours quite cold, and my nose were not within a foot of the body, yet there came out so quick and penetrating a steam, that it made me cry out, and made my eyes run over."

Oxford as a scientific centre was gradually coming to be appreciated abroad in the earlier 1660's, thanks above all to Boyle. Claus Borrichius (1626–90), the Danish chemist, writing in 1663, mentioned with approval the chemical avocations of Oxford, but it was not without a wry smile that he commented that one of these pundits believed that iron could dissolve by itself without the presence of an acid, while another stated that "the whole substance of water, but only after a long lapse of time, changes into earth like chalk."

Although Boyle stayed in Oxford until 1668, many members of the "experimental philosophical club" returned to London at the time of the Restoration. They left a great gap in the University, but its loss was England's gain, for by 1662 the Royal Society was established.

Not all Oxford's scientists went, however, and of those who remained John Mayow (1643–79), fellow of All Souls, was outstanding. His experiments, all carried out in Oxford, though where is not precisely known, were explained in his *Tractatus de Respiratione* (1668). It was no less than an account of oxygen and nitrogen. Air, Mayow maintained, was a mixture of two gases: *spiritus nitro-aereus*, the one (oxygen, *spiritus*) necessary to life and kindling, the other (nitrogen, *nitro-aereus*) not supporting life or flame. In another treatise, *Tractatus Quinque Medico-physici* (1674), he elaborated on this matter, besides pointing out the importance of nitrates in agriculture.

In the first essay in the latter book, "De sal-nitro et spiritu nitro-aereo," Mayow showed that oxygen (*spiritus*) was to be found in saltpetre and proved that without it acids would not have corrosive power and gunpowder would not be an explosive. His remarkable discoveries of acids and oxides were then illustrated. He heated antimony placed in a glass flask or jar with air in it. By using a lens and focusing sunlight on the antimony, he burned it to a calx and then noticed that the calx increased in weight while the volume of air lessened. His conclusion was that the increased weight was due to "the fixation of something in the air." Other experiments with sulphuric acid, nitric acid, and pyrites only confirmed his surmise. What in fact Mayow had done was nothing less than to have grasped the essential facts about acids and oxides, anticipating Lavoisier by a hundred years.

In 1675, Oxford's greatest chemist left the University for Bath to practice medicine, thus passing out of view.

Mayow's work was unappreciated in his lifetime and was soon forgotten when the phlogiston theory became the accepted ground belief of scientists. If, instead of following Stahl's faulty explanation, great chemists like Joseph Priestley and Henry Cavendish had glanced at Mayow's work, eighteenth-century chemistry in England would have had more rewarding results. It was not until 1790 that Thomas Beddoes and others began his rehabilitation, calling him "the father of pneumatic chemistry."

Some of the Oxford scientists were practical inventors. John Aubrey in his *Brief Lives* tells us that Francis Potter (1594–1678) of Trinity gave his attention to hydraulics and was responsible for a water engine for drawing water from the deepest wells. A sketch made by Aubrey of this engine is preserved in the Bodleian Library. John Wilkins is credited with a plan for a flying machine and the invention of a wind gun. It was, however, Christopher Wren and Robert Hooke who were the glory of Oxford mechanics, improvements to carriages, the theory of impact, the pendulum, and the theory of velocity being amongst many other matters due to them.

Experiments on pendulums—and Hooke revolutionised the designs of clocks and of watches too, for he it was who invented the circular pendulum—led to the idea of measuring the force of gravity by swinging them. Hooke seems to have been responsible for this also, in 1666 being able to show by experiment that "the centre of gravity of the earth and moon is the point describing an ellipse round the sun." Wren was busy enquiring into every kind of mechanical subject, such as the laws of motion, the problem of navigation, and the velocity and power of water.

86

The breadth of Wren's interests can be seen in *A Catalogue of New Theories, Inventions, Experiments and Mechanic Improvements, exhibited by Mr. Wren, at the first Assemblies at WADHAM-COLLEGE in Oxford, for Advancement of Natural and Experimental Knowledge . . .* , from which one can realise that his inventions included a weather wheel and weather clock, a balance, artificial eyes, a perspective box, and false marble, and that he was actively engaged in trying to invent a means of turning salt water into fresh water at sea, designing submarines, and discovering ways of blasting rocks in mining, besides improving musical instruments and engaging in cartography and printing.

Wren's fame was spreading, and soon foreigners, like the Frenchman Monconys, were coming to Oxford to visit him. Monconys in his *Voyage d'Angleterre* (1666) vividly describes his meeting with Wren ("M. Renes") in June, 1663. What particularly impressed him were Wren's meteorological instruments, especially his weather clock, thermometer, and rain gauge. Certainly meteorology was one of Wren's particular interests at this time. As he explained to the Royal Society, weather diaries should be kept by people in different parts of the country, from which could be drawn up observations, and thus in time might be established a law of seasons and a pattern of weather conditions at various periods of the year.

With the keeping of such a diary in mind, Wren invented a special thermometer and anemometer, to which latter a clock was attached, "which moved a rundle covered with white paper; upon which the clock moving a black-lead pencil, the observer, by the traces on the paper, may certainly know what winds have blown, during his sleep or absence, for 12 hours together." It was Robert Hooke who actually made the model of Wren's weather clock with improvements of his own in 1664. The outstanding point of Wren's originality in this instrument was the revolving drum and pencil. Practically all self-recording instruments, including seismographs and barometers, are so designed, and from this the system of present-day radiographs with their arms and turntables may be said to be descended. Wren also increased the efficiency of hygrometers and barometers.

Here Boyle must again be introduced as a pioneer in meteorology, and his *History of Cold* (1665) is a classic. John Wallis, using a barometer invented by Boyle, kept readings for six years. John Locke himself caught the meteorologic fever and, using a thermoscope, a barometer filled with mercury, and a homemade hydroscope—nothing but a wild-oat awn—kept a register in which he recorded weather, wind, moisture, temperature, and atmospheric pressure in Oxford in 1666–67 and 1681–82 and for a few days in June, 1683. Hooke invented three kinds of barometers, the marine, the double, and the wheel, and also the cup anemometer.

Oxford in Locke's day was also a nursery for astronomy, and it deserved to be. The Savilian Chair of Astronomy had first been occupied by John Bainbridge (1582–1643), but he appears to have carried out little or no practical work and probably had few instruments at his command. The accomplishments of the second Savilian professor were very different, for John Greaves (1602–52) was a practical astronomer with his own collection of sextants, quadrants,

telescopes, astrolabes, globes, and clocks, which are listed
as having been given to the Museum Savilianum by him
and his brother Thomas, deputy reader in Arabic in the
University. Greaves made his observations from the tower
of the Examination Schools, and one must think of him
winding his way up the spiral staircase, lit by a servant
carrying a wavering candle, on many a cold, damp night
during the anxious Civil War years.

We know little or nothing of what Greaves actually
discovered, if anything, and he had little time to do much,
for he was deprived of his chair as a Royalist, and it was
Seth Ward, Savilian Professor from 1649 to 1661, who is
generally considered the first Oxford astronomer of importance since the time of Thomas Lydiat, a fellow of
New College in the earlier sixteenth century, known for
his proposed revisions for a new calendar. Ward's celebrity
was founded on his theory of the orbits of comets, which
agrees with modern ideas. The great Kepler had maintained that they were no more than objects which burned
themselves out and vanished; others, disbelieving this
theory, held that, far from being self-consuming, they
were *corpora aeterna* passing the earth in straight lines
never to return.

Ward, on the other hand, in a lecture published in
1653 stated (to quote from Robert Plot's *Oxfordshire*)
that comets were "carried round in circles or ellipses
(either including or excluding the globe of the Earth) so
great, that the comets are never visible to us but when
they come to the perigees of those circles or ellipses, and
ever after invisible till they have absolved their periods
in those vast orbs, which by reason of their standing in an

89

oblique or perpendicular posture to the eye . . . might well seem to carry them in straight lines; all circles or ellipses so posited, projecting themselves naturally into such lines."

Ward's astronomical work was continued by Robert Holland, a "teacher" of mathematics in Oxford, the results of his labours (that on the parallax of comets being especially notable) appearing in two books, *Notes on how to get the Angle of Parallax of a Comet* (1668) and *Globe Notes* (1678).

Astronomy also held a prime position among Wren's multifarious pursuits. While still an undergraduate at Wadham (the leading scientific college in the mid-seventeenth century) he made observations of Saturn, in 1655 attempting to construct a wax model of the planet; made researches into methods for discovering the longitude at sea; formulated a theory of the moon's libration; and investigated Descartes' theory of the moon's pressure on the sea which was the cause of tides.

In 1657, Wren left Oxford, where he had been fellow of All Souls since 1653, to take up the appointment of Professor of Astronomy at Gresham College, London; but in 1661 he returned to his Alma Mater, succeeding Ward in the Savilian Chair, a position which he held until 1673, when he resigned it, finding it impossible to combine his academic work with his highly important London position of Surveyor of the King's Works. By 1665 architecture was beginning to exclude all other interests, and his visit to Paris in that year, during which time he gave practically all his attention to studying French buildings and building methods, increased that tendency. In

1669 he presented to Oxford his first great architectural achievements, the Sheldonian Theatre, ever afterwards used for University ceremonies. Already, however, in astronomy, physics, meteorology, and mathematics he had by his remarkable gifts helped to carry Oxford's scientific fame to the Continent, especially to France and the United Provinces of the Netherlands, where Christian Huygens, that notable astronomer and mathematician, acknowledged him as an equal.

Even as Wren turned aside from astronomy, a worthy successor in this field was studying in Oxford. Edmund Halley (1656–1742), of comet fame and in due time to occupy the Savilian Chair (1703), entered Queen's College, Oxford, in 1673 (the very year that Wren severed his official connection with his University) and while still an undergraduate observed and recorded a sunspot and an occultation of Mars.

Yet Oxford for all its scientific liveliness had for the greater part of Locke's time in the University no proper building in which to house instruments and books and in which scientific teaching might be held worthily and un-interruptedly. That came in 1683 with the completion of the Ashmolean Chemical Laboratory, a year which also saw the setting up of similar edifices in Germany at Altdorf and in Sweden at Stockholm.

The construction of the Ashmolean Museum has already been described. It also belongs to this *annus mirabilis*. In March, 1683, the whole Ashmolean building was finished. It consisted of three storeys. In the upper was the Ashmolean Museum itself; in the middle was the School of Natural History, in which lectures were to be held; while below that and extending into the cellar was the Officina Chymica, the laboratory, to which was attached a storeroom.

Elias Ashmole would be sorry to think that his name is now in the general mind associated with the University Museum and Art Gallery, since it commemorates only part of his plan. He was as desirous as the University authorities to encourage science and give it a proper habitation. The Old Ashmolean in Broad Street, far from being the secluded place it is now, from 1683 onwards for a century and a half was the hive of activity that Ashmole intended.

We have a record, dated 1683, of the cost of fitting up the chemical laboratory:

	£.	s.	d.
To Wood the Stonecutter for work done at the Laboratory	106	17	4
To Thomas Robinson the mason for work done there simlr	31	2	4
To Job Dew Plaisterer for work done there	1	16	0
To William Longe & John White Carpenters, simlr	23	14	7
Payd to Dr. Plott [curator] what he has laid out for some vessels etc. for the Laboratory	17	9	0
To Chr. White Tin Copper & Iron Vessels simlr	44	17	0

Before the middle of the year the laboratory was being used for experiments. In May the Duke of York [afterwards James II] and his family visited the building, and Anthony à Wood described the visit. After being received by Dr. Plot, Keeper and University Reader in Chemistry, and being shown the Museum, they were entertained at a banquet. "Then they went down to the elaboratory, where they saw some experiments to their great satisfaction." The laboratory was described by Wood as "perchance one of the most beautiful and useful in the world, furnished with all sorts of furnaces and all other necessary materials in order to use and practice."

The *"chymical librarie,"* already described, which the Ashmolean contained, was of the greatest consequence in the furthering of that science, as was "the store-room for Chymical preparations."

It is interesting to notice that the design of the Ashmolean Laboratory was followed in the planning of the laboratory of the University of Utrecht in 1698. Each had a stone vault as a precaution against fire, and each had a furnace placed against one wall, with a metal hood, which was considered a great improvement on the older design of having the furnaces grouped round a central chimney, their several flues converging on the stack in the middle.

The Ashmolean Laboratory at once became the focal point of Oxford science, and by the autumn of 1683 courses and discussions, patronised by senior members of the University, were firmly established. By December a similar curriculum had been inaugurated at Trinity College, Dublin, and its *conventus* regularly corresponded with the Oxford scientists.

Thus it can be seen that in Locke's day Oxford was, scientifically speaking, very much alive and a centre of activities recognised not only in England but on the Continent, where its influence was felt.

V

John Locke at Oxford

In 1652 at age twenty Locke became an Oxford undergraduate just at the time of John Owen's appointment as
Vice-Chancellor and Dean of Christ Church. It was the
very moment of the start of the attempted Puritan reformation of the University. Locke was thus plunged into
a world of increasingly high endeavour and into the very
college, Christ Church, which in the past had been the
richest and most influential of all in Oxford.

As we have seen, the Commonwealth period at Oxford
had many good features, and Oliver Cromwell and
Fairfax had the essential well-being of the academic community at heart. Discipline was enforced as never before
since pre-Reformation days, while the tutor's position became as important and multifarious as it had not been for

over a century and was not to be again for nearly two
hundred years. The college tutor in fact not only per
formed his academic duties to his charges exactly but also
took a keen interest in their spiritual welfare.

Locke's tutor was Thomas Cole, who was his senior by
not more than half a dozen years and who like his pupi
had been a scholar of Westminster School. Ordained in
the Church of England, he had abandoned his orders to
become an Independent minister, and in 1656 was chosen
Principal of St. Mary Hall. With the Restoration of
1660 he was ejected from his Oxford post and was forced
to open a private school for the sons of Independents at
Nettlebed, an Oxfordshire village. Ultimately he settled
in London, where he died in 1697. He was a kindly, tol
erant man and an excellent scholar of whom even such
Anglicans and Royalists as Anthony à Wood approved,
terming him "a man of good learning and of a gentle
spirit." How far he influenced Locke it is difficult to de
cide. We certainly hear of no intimacy between them, but
he seems to have directed the young undergraduate's
reading with benevolent firmness, keeping him in mind
of college and University discipline from day to day.

That brings us to the question of how Locke lived at
Oxford. His day would begin at five o'clock in the morning with attendance at chapel, where, of course, the ritual
and liturgy of the Church of England had been displaced
by a form of worship in accordance with the rule of the
Westminster Assembly. Breakfast followed the service,
and between then and the midday dinner he attended
University and college lectures, having prepared for them
under Cole's guidance. During dinner such conversation

96

s was allowed was held in Latin. After the meal another
compulsory lecture generally followed, and then he was
free to attend or absent himself as he wished from University Acts,—oral examinations sustained by those who
were going through courses leading to the degree of bachelor of arts. On Thursdays and Saturdays the schedule
varied; on Thursdays he must have attended the Christ
Church sermon at four o'clock, and on Saturday afternoons he prepared for the devotions of the Sabbath.

We know that Locke thoroughly disliked the University Acts, which he found irksome in the extreme, according to his friend James Tyrrell, who so reported to
Lady Masham, in whose house Locke spent his later years.
After his death Jean le Clerc, the famous savant and
Locke's close companion when he was in Amsterdam,
asked for biographical information about him. Lady
Masham answered in a letter of January 12, 1705, quoting
Tyrrell: "Mr. Locke never loved the trade of disputing in
public in the schools, but was always wont to declaim
against it as being invented for wrangling or ostentation,
rather than to discover truth."

With the end of the afternoon's work there was still
much to be done. There was an evening service to attend
in Christ Church Cathedral, which, as it still does, served
also as the college chapel, and even after that he had to
go to his tutor's study, together with his fellow undergraduates, to hear prayers and to give a full account of
what he had done during the day. Then at last he was
free—but not for long, since bedtime was early—to relax
within college or go for an innocent walk with his tutor's
permission.

If we wish to find out more about the formal lecture Locke must have attended during his undergraduate years we cannot do better than look into Wood's *Fast Oxonienses*, in which we are told that during the first and second years there were four lectures a week. In the first year the scholar attended lectures on rhetoric every Monday and Thursday morning and on grammar every Tuesday and Friday morning. In the second year his Monday and Thursday morning lectures were devoted to logic delivered by a fellow of his own college, while the Tuesday and Friday morning sessions were on moral philosophy, delivered by the University professor of that subject. Other and more elementary subjects and those such as Greek, Latin, and a modicum of Hebrew (in which he would already have had a good grounding while at school at Westminster), were not touched on by the lecturers and were studied under his tutor's supervision.

In the third year the Monday and Thursday lectures on logic continued, as also the Tuesday and Friday ones on moral philosophy, while four more were added—those on geometry on Wednesday and Saturday mornings and on Greek in the afternoon of those days.

In the fourth and final year the same round of eight weekly lectures on the same subjects continued, and in addition it was time for him to "argue on themes" in Latin in public with his fellow students. Such was Locke's timetable until February 14, 1656, when he graduated with the degree of bachelor of arts.

This dry intellectual diet can hardly have been much to Locke's taste, and Tyrrell corroborates this conclusion. The logic course, "debased Aristotelianism," one might call it, must have been a dead one, in spite of the so-called reforms in it which had in the previous century been carried out by the Huguenot logician Pierre de la Ramée (known as Peter Ramus, 1515–72) and which in Locke's time were adopted in Oxford. Francis Bacon had a generation before complained that watered-down Aristotelianism had reduced "the gravest of sciences [logic] to childish sophistry and ridiculous affectation"; and although Oxford had paid lip service to the great moral and natural philosopher, "a mighty Hercules," the pseudo-Aristotelian pillars of Oxford logic remained. In fact, Locke himself was later to write in his *Thoughts concerning Education* (1693) : "I have seldom or never observed any one to get the skill of reasoning well or speaking handsomely by studying those rules which pretend to teach it."

Among those whose lectures Locke attended were Henry Wilkinson, a Presbyterian, and Francis Howell, an Independent. The subject of both lecturers was moral philosophy, but Howell was much better known and succeeded to the professorship in 1654. Both men had the reputation for liberality in religious views, but nothing of this welcome moderate tendency was to be heard in their dry expositions of Aristotle, on whose works, such as the *Politics*, *Nicomachean Ethics*, and *Economics*, they were forced to discourse.

Locke seems to have withered under that barren discipline and to have almost rebelled. In fact, he was often looked upon in Oxford circles in the years to come as of a quarrelsome nature and angular in character, which was by no means his true self, but was probably produced by exasperation at the narrow academic bounds which

99

hedged him in. As his benefactress Lady Masham was to write to Jean le Clerc in the letter of 1705, quoted earlier:

"I have often heard him say, in reference to his first years spent in the university, that he had so small satisfaction there from his studies, as finding very little light brought thereby to his understanding, that he became discontented with his manner of life, and wished his father had rather designed him for anything else, than what he was destined to." Jean le Clerc himself in the *Éloge de M. Locke* in his *Bibliothèque Choisie* wrote:

"I myself heard him complain of his early studies . . ., and when I told him that I had a tutor who was a disciple of Descartes and was a man of very clear intelligence, he said that he had not that good fortune . . . and that he lost a great deal of time at the beginning of his studies, because the only philosophy then known at Oxford was the peripatetic, overlaid with obscure terms and useless questions."

So far so bad for Locke; but when in his third year his studies broadened, he seized with relief the opportunity to read geometry under that excellent and lively exponent John Wallis, Savilian Professor of Geometry from 1649 until his death in 1703. Wallis was one of those wide-ranging geniuses which one associates with seventeenth-century culture. There was nothing of the dreary schoolman about him, and his influence on his pupils was great. Locke was indeed fortunate in being one of them. On Wednesdays and Saturdays, Wallis lectured formally, but he also had an informal class in his own lodgings which was particularly appreciated, since at that time anything might be discussed. Wallis's interpretation of geometry by no means confined him exactly to that subject, and even in those formal lectures on Wednesdays and Saturdays he dealt with logic, mechanics, and even the principles of music.

It was his master's teaching of logic which Locke seems especially to have valued, and in his *Thoughts concerning Education* there are echoes of Wallis' own views, such as, for example, Locke's reference to arithmetic: "Arithmetic is the easiest and consequently the first sort of abstract reasoning which the mind commonly bears or accustoms itself to"; or to Greek, which, as did Wallis, Locke regarded in a practical way: "Amongst the Grecians is to be found the original, as it were, and foundation of all that learning which we have in this part of the world. I grant it so; and will add that no man can pass for a scholar that is ignorant of the Greek tongue. But I am not here considering of the education of a professed scholar, but of a gentleman, to whom Latin and French, as the world now goes, is by everyone acknowledged to be necessary." In other words, no learning must be mere pedantry. With such views it is hardly surprising that Locke had little regard for the lectures of John Harmar, Regius Professor of Greek from 1650 to 1660, whose reputation, as Wood describes it in *Athenae Oxonienses*, was founded on his ability to translate "Greek into Latin, or Latin into English, or English into Greek or Latin, whether in prose or verse." Harmar was in fact particularly well known for his translation of Butler's *Hudibras*, work which Wallis and Locke condemned as time-wasting vanity.

As we have seen, Locke graduated as bachelor of arts

in February, 1656, and became master of arts in June, 1658. Although there is no record of the fact, he was soon afterwards elected to a senior studentship (fellowship) at Christ Church. He was not, however, the man to sit back, like so many of his contemporaries, and simply enjoy his benefice. Though he was not legally bound to work, morally he felt compelled to do so. The seeds of his new interests were sown during the period between 1656 and 1658, when he was preparing for the master's degree, for while he had such dry reading to carry out as Aristotle's logic, metaphysics, and moral and natural philosophy (what we would call physics), he also had to read history, both classical and early mediaeval, according to the *Shaftesbury Papers*. Of history Locke was later to write in *Thoughts concerning Education*: "As nothing teaches, so nothing delights more than history," for he was always interested in men, and soon he was to find his proper place beyond the bounds of a college and out in the wide world. So he attended the lectures of Lewis du Moulin, "a most violent nonconformist," who was Camden Professor of Ancient History for twelve years until he lost his post at the Restoration in 1660.

It was at this time also that Locke went to Ward's courses on astronomy, which embraced lectures on ancient methods of astronomy from Ptolemy onwards, the Copernican system, Galileo, optics, gnomonics (the science of dialling), and the use of mathematics in navigation and geography. Locke did not turn into another Newton, and it is well that the two great minds of the age did not develop in the same direction; but under Ward he learned to speak in the language of the new sciences and was enabled in the future to communicate with scientists in their own parlance.

Furthermore, in order to be able to qualify for the master's degree, he was expected to learn some Arabic and more Hebrew. He seems to have had little interest in Oriental languages, but his enforced attendance at the lectures led him to make the acquaintance of one of the greatest scholars of the age, that man of sterling character, Edward Pococke, Regius Professor of Hebrew and Laudian Professor of Arabic, the man whom of all his Oxford masters Locke most admired.

Pococke (1604–91) was the son of an Oxford clergyman. Educated at Corpus Christi College, he became a fellow there and shortly afterwards took the opportunity of going to the East by becoming chaplain to the English merchants at Aleppo in 1629. There he made good use of his time, gaining a wonderful knowledge of Arabic, and he was also commissioned by Archbishop Laud to buy Oriental manuscripts. On his return he was rewarded by being made the first Laudian Professor of Arabic, and after a short period he set out for the Middle East again to procure manuscripts.

On his return to England, however, Pococke found that the Civil War had broken out and that Laud was a prisoner in the Tower of London. He lost his professorship for a time as a well-known Royalist, but, thanks to the influence of the antiquary John Selden, it was restored to him in 1648, and he was given the Chair of Hebrew as well. He translated Hugo Grotius' *De Veritate* into Arabic, and among his many other works one might mention *Specimen Historiae Arabum*, a poem of his own in Arabic entitled *Carmen Abu Ismaelis Tograi,* and an Arabic translation of the liturgy and catechism of the Church of England. As a Hebrew scholar he is best represented by *Porta Mosis; or, Six Discourses of Maimonides* and his *Commentary on Micah, Malachi, Hosea and Joel.*

What struck Locke even more than Pococke's scholarship was his very attractive nature, and it is not too much to say that Pococke's example had a lasting effect on his pupil. Everyone who met Locke was struck by his charming and unaffected manners, but few knew how he had had to discipline himself and gain control of an easily roused temper. His guiding star was Pococke, of whom he was later to write enthusiastically: "So extraordinary an example in so degenerate an age deserves, for the rarity, and, I was going to say, for the incredibility of it, the attestation of all that knew him, and considered his worth." At the very end of his life Locke still wrote of Pococke with the same warmth, as is to be seen in this letter to his friend Humphrey Smith in 1703:

"He was a man of no irregular appetites. If he indulged any one too much, it was that of study, which his wife would often complain of (I think not without reason), that a due consideration of his age and health could not make him abate. Though he was a man of the greatest temperance in himself, and the farthest from ostentation and vanity in his way of living, yet he was of a liberal mind and given to hospitality, which, considering the smallness of his preferments and the numerous family of children he had to provide for, might be thought to have outdone those who made more noise and show. I do not remember that in all my conversation with him I ever saw him once angry. . . . His life appeared to me one constant calm. I can say of him, what few men can say of any friend of theirs, nor I of any other of my acquaintance, that I do not remember I ever saw in him any one action that I did or could, in my own mind, blame or think amiss in him."

Pococke, the great Royalist and episcopalian, who may be said to have weaned Locke from the Puritanism inherited from his family, takes his place beside Wallis and Ward as a beneficent influence.

What of Locke's friendships among his contemporaries at Oxford? He had three: Nathaniel Hodges, David Thomas, and James Tyrrell. Hodges left Westminster and entered Christ Church, Oxford, in the same year that Locke entered the school. Later Hodges was befriended by the Earl of Shaftesbury (probably thanks to Locke), and gained Church preferment. Although they appear to have seen little of one another in later years, Locke did not forget Hodges. Writing to Edward Clarke in 1700 he says: "I hear, this post that my old friend Mr. Hodges is dead. He, Dr. Thomas, and I were intimate friends in our younger days in the university. They two are gone, and who could have thought that I much the weakest and most unlikely of the three, should have outlived them?"

David Thomas was educated at New College, Oxford, became doctor of medicine in 1670, and thereafter practised in his native Salisbury. Both Hodges and Thomas were a good deal older than Locke. The third friend, James Tyrrell, was ten years younger, having been born in 1642 in London, the eldest son of Sir Timothy Tyrrell of Shotover, near Oxford. Tyrrell's mother was the daughter of the famous Archbishop James Ussher. He was at Queen's, from which he took his degree of master of arts in 1663, and two years later he was called to the bar, though he never practised as a barrister. He divided his time between London and the house at Shotover, which he inherited, occupying himself chiefly in literary work, which resulted in such books as *Bibliotheca Politica*, *Brief Disquisition on the Laws of Nature*, and above all the *History of England*.

Locke had not long settled down to his Christ Church studentship (fellowship) when in 1660 came the Restoration. But the new regime did not repeat the sweeping policy of the Puritans a dozen years before. Apart from the replacement of intruded heads of colleges by Royalists there was little interference with the personnel, and most fellows, even though they had gained their positions thanks to the Cromwellians, were left alone.

Among the new heads was one whose influence on the University was of the greatest importance and one with whom Locke must have come into frequent contact. He was John Fell, the new Dean of Christ Church, soon to be Vice-Chancellor, under whose stern eye order and discipline were brought back to Oxford after several unsettled years. As Stephen Penton, already mentioned, was later to write of the Restoration period in Oxford in *The Guardians Instructor, or the Gentlemans Romance* (1688) :

"To study was fanaticism; to be moderate was downright rebellion; . . . and thus it would have continued till this time if it had not pleased God to raise up some vice-chancellor who stemmed the torrent which carried so much filth with it, and . . . reduced the university to that temperament that a man might study and not be thought a dullard, might be sober and yet a conformist, a scholar and yet a Church of England man; and from that time the University became sober, modest, and studious as perhaps any university in Europe."

Locke was glad to see the change, for he had already had enough of the uncertainties and troubles which had grown up during the last two years of Presbyterian rule. He returned to Oxford, after a period of absence caused by the illness and death of his father, towards the end of 1660 and was immediately appointed lecturer and tutor in Greek.

Christ Church had remained the leading Oxford college during the 1650's, and the new Dean, John Fell, was determined that this position should be not only maintained but improved. As Mallet in his *History of the University of Oxford* says: "[Fell] was determined that even the young bloods . . . should work. He would visit them in their rooms and examine them in their studies. . . . He revived the attendance at lectures and disputations. He would often be present at examinations. He would, if necessary, intervene to conduct an examination himself. He stopped the practice of coursing and the tumults which it led to. . . . Not content with the moral improvement of his college, Fell saw to it that its architectural appearance was improved. He appealed to old members, and so great was the response that he was able to have the main quadrangle completed—it had stood unfinished for over a century—by the building of the north side. . . ." He was also responsible for the erection of Tom Tower, the well-known gatehouse tower designed by Wren.

Locke's tutorial work was not onerous, and he seems never to have had more than ten pupils at one time. Other small college offices came his way during the next year or two, such as the readership in rhetoric and the censorship of moral philosophy; but since he sought nothing, so he gained nothing else. Until 1666 he at various times considered taking holy orders, but then he decided on medicine, for he was becoming more and more involved in science, thanks above all to the influence of Robert Boyle. Boyle's approach to science was the same as Locke's: neither looked on science with preconceived metaphysical (one would at this period say Cartesian) ideas, and both made it their goal to be pure scientists.

Yet still at the back of his mind Locke held his tendency towards the Church, and it was in this quandary that he turned to his childhood friend John Strachey, now a prosperous Somerset squire. When Locke had first known him, Strachey had slight prospects in the world, but afterward, owing to a train of good fortune which he in no wise deserved, he had reached success. Locke, having been out of touch with him for some time, naturally believed that his phenomenal rise to good estate had resulted from his own abilities and turned to him for advice. Writing to his old friend, he posed to him the great question, Should he take holy orders? Strachey replied as directly, Certainly not! and added that it would be far better to go abroad for a year or so. After a period of indecision Locke decided to follow Strachey's advice.

He obtained a diplomatic post, probably through the influence of William Godolphin, a leading figure in the Foreign Office, and it is possible that Locke had become personally acquainted with Charles II when the King stayed in Oxford with the Court during the plague in the autumn of 1665 and lodged in Christ Church.

Godolphin, older brother of the much more famous Sydney Godolphin (afterwards Lord High Treasurer), had been at school with Locke and was also a contemporary of his at Christ Church, but their interests had separated them in their undergraduate days. While Locke was busy with intellectual pursuits, Godolphin was actively interested in politics, serving as a Royalist agent for another old member of Westminster School and Christ Church, Sir Henry Bennet (later Earl of Arlington), who had been in Europe with the exiled royal family. After the Restoration, Godolphin gained his reward, becoming Member of Parliament in 1661 and soon afterward private secretary to Bennet, who had become Secretary of State and almost equal in position to Lord Chancellor Clarendon, the most powerful man in the country. In fact, Bennet and Anthony Ashley-Cooper profited from Clarendon's loss of popularity owing to the reactionary tendencies of the Parliament of 1661, and were regarded as the hope of a more liberal policy. It was they who forced on the King the Declaration of Indulgence at the end of 1662, impressing on him that only in such a way could he allay public suspicion aroused by the judicial murder of Sir Henry Vane and the harsh treatment meted out to the Nonconformists.

Altogether, so carefully did the High Church and reactionary party behave during the early years of Charles II's reign—Vane's execution was excused as the result of the King's natural eagerness to avenge his father's death—that the nation in general, Locke amongst them, did not feel particular dissatisfaction with the new government and hoped for better things.

Locke was no cloistered recluse, and that visit of the Court to Christ Church in 1665 drove him on to his ambition of cutting a figure in a wider world. In November of that year he left England as secretary to a diplomatic mission to Brandenburg, an important mission, since, with England at war with the United Provinces of the Netherlands, it was necessary for Charles II to win such an ally as the friendly Elector of Brandenburg, or at any rate to make certain of his neutrality.

The mission succeeded. It was a pleasant interlude for Locke, but the next year he was back in Oxford, eager to follow a systematic study of medicine, which he hoped he would be able to pursue while engaged in his philosophical and scientific interests and which in the future might lead him to a tangible profession, should he need one. Besides, although owing to the confusions of the times, when he became a senior student, he had in no way been pressed to take holy orders as a condition for continuing in his college post (since he did not hold one of the five studentships open to laymen, but one of the other fifty-five open to clerics only), there was no knowing when the matter might not be brought up, and he wanted to make an end of the uncertainty.

It seems at first sight extraordinary that a man of his ability failed in his plan to become an Oxford doctor of medicine; but then that is to forget a less-well-known side of Locke's character, for behind all his apparent placidity he was stubborn and a rebel. From the first he despised orthodox medicine and laughed at the Oxford requirements for medical degrees, being especially impatient of the rules for attendance at lectures for the degree of bachelor of medicine.

It must be admitted that the course for the baccalaureate was tedious (and Thomas Sydenham, the greatest physician of the day, who soon became Locke's friend, heartily concurred with this view) and pedantic in the extreme; but there it was, and many were ready to go through with it in order to reap the benefits later. Not so Locke. Why should he attend for three years lectures on Arabic for the purpose of learning such outworn stuff as Avicenna's *Canon of Medicine*, that medical Bible of the Middle Ages on anatomy and on medicine? And yet, if one followed these courses and took part in some disputations in the medical school, one would soon obtain the baccalaureate and four years later gain the doctorate without much ado. Lectures on medicine were given twice a week during term, but they went no further than Hippocrates and Galen. Anatomy amounted to dissecting one human body and attending four lectures on the dissection, followed by three more lectures on the human skeleton. But in Locke's time the Regius Professor of Medicine was too busy with his lucrative London practice to come to Oxford, and so his deputy carried out his duties. This was a pity, for Dr. James Hyde might well have roused Locke's interest, to a certain extent at any rate; but his deputy certainly did not, and the Hippocratic diet was too dry for his appetite.

Having set his heart against the bachelor's course, Locke tried to bypass it, and, realising that it would be useless to appeal to the University authorities to grant him the doctorate at once, he turned to Anthony Ashley-Cooper, whom he had met the previous summer (1666) while he himself was a diplomatic secretary in Brandenburg. Ashley at once asked Chancellor Clarendon to make the request for the bestowal of the doctorate to the academic officials on Locke's behalf. Clarendon complied and at the beginning of November addressed this letter to them:

"Mr. Vice-Chancellor and Gentlemen,

"I am very well assured that Mr. John Locke, a Master of Arts and Student of Christ Church, has employed his time in the study of physic [medicine] to so good purpose that he is in all respects qualified for the degree of Doctor in that faculty; . . . but not having taken the degree of bachelor of physic, he has desired that he may be dispensed with to accummulate to that degree [to take the bachelor's and doctor's degrees in medicine at the same time], which appears to me a very modest and reasonable request, he professing himself ready to perform the exercises for both degrees. I therefore give my consent that a dispensation to that purpose be propounded for him. . . ."

Although this letter came from England's most powerful statesman, the Oxford Faculty of Medicine chose to ignore it. They were not thus to be dictated to, and be-

sides Locke was already beginning to make enemies, enemies who in 1684 were to have his name removed forever
from the roll of Christ Church's senior students. The High
Church party was firmly in power in Westminster and in
Oxford, and Locke was only too well known to be fa-
voured by such a liberal as Ashley. The request failed,
and Locke obtained no medical degree whatever, and was
not to gain anything in that line until he became a
bachelor of medicine in 1675. He never proceeded to the
doctorate.

For the moment, however, he was much more troubled
about his very studentship, for he had no intention of
taking holy orders. Seeing that he had enemies in Oxford, might it not be possible that they would bring this
against him and try to oust him from his benefice? It was
necessary for him to have a supporting letter, and he
sought one from the King himself. This time the letter
was successful; how could it be otherwise? It was King
Charles's command addressed to the Dean and Chapter
of Christ Church:

"Trusty and well-beloved, we greet you well.
"Whereas we are informed that John Locke, Master
of Arts and Student of Christ Church in our university
of Oxford, is of such standing [academic seniority] as by
the custom of that college he is obliged to enter into holy
orders or otherwise to leave his Student's place there; at
his humble request that he may still have the further
time to prosecute his studies without that obligation, we
are graciously pleased to grant him our royal dispensation, and do accordingly hereby require you to suffer him,

the said John Locke, to hold and enjoy his said Student's place in Christ Church, together with all the rights, profits, and emoluments thereunto belonging, without taking holy orders upon him according to the custom of the college or any rule of the Students in that case, with which we are graciously pleased to dispense in that behalf. And for so doing this shall be your warrant. Given at our Court at Whitehall, the 14th day of November, 1666, in the eighteenth year of our reign. . . ."

This dispensation, which was signed by William Morrice, Secretary of State, put an end to all Locke's difficulties on that score. He could now enjoy every advantage of his studentship with all the backing of royal authority and could afford to snap his fingers at University and college officials. Having been snubbed by them over his attempt to gain his doctorate in medicine, he refused to teach any more and by the beginning of 1667 had ceased to be a college tutor. As appears from a passage in a letter he wrote at this time to Boyle, he was preparing to leave Oxford, possibly permanently. He wrote on February 24, 1667:

"I intend to go between this and Easter into Somersetshire. . . . It is so much my concernment to receive your commands, that I shall be sure to give you notice where I am and how I may receive the honour of your letters. After some little stay in that country I hope to kiss your hands in London."

Then in the spring came Ashley's invitation to Locke to live with him in London as his physician. This invitation proved decisive. Any doubts Locke may have had were swept away. In the metropolis he could find every-thing he missed in Oxford, and there the Royal Society flourished, drawing away from the University the greater part of its scientific talent. Boyle, Willis, and Sydenham were all in London; there he would be free from carping academics, out in the wide world far from the musty schoolmen.

By the early summer of 1667 he was packing, having let his rooms in Christ Church, and on June 15 was at Ashley's town residence, Exeter House in the Strand. "From that time," Lady Masham was to write to Jean le Clerc in 1705, "he was with my Lord Ashley as a man at home, and lived in that family much esteemed, not only by my lord, but by all the friends of the family."

For the moment Locke's connection with Oxford was of the slenderest. In 1669 a new attempt was made by Ashley to gain the doctorate in medicine for him. Claren-don was no longer Chancellor of the University, and it was to his successor, the Duke of Ormonde, that he ap-plied. William, Prince of Orange, was to be entertained at Oxford before long, and some honorary degrees were to be given on the occasion. Ormonde agreed, and a letter to the Vice-Chancellor appears to have been drafted, but it seems never to have been sent, for Locke, having realised that the High Church party at Oxford was still as strong against him as ever, asked for it to be cancelled.

Locke had reason to dislike the University now, but if it was not good for his career, it was good for his health. He paid a visit to Oxford in 1670. His lungs were troubling him, as they were to do throughout his life. Neither Lon-don nor Somerset air was satisfactory; but at Oxford, he wrote to a friend: "I mended apace, and my cough sensibly abated." But he did not stay there long and was soon back in the bosom of the Ashley family in London.

It was not until the end of 1679 that Locke again took up residence in Oxford. He seems to have been there in May of that year, but only for a short visit whose purpose was political, for his patron Ashley, now Earl of Shaftesbury, was deeply involved. He was entering the last round in his defiance of King and Court. Charles II, in spite of many a French bribe, was running short of money and, believing that it would be easier to browbeat Parliament if it met outside London, ordered it to meet in Oxford in May, 1679. Two months' wrangling was sufficient to show that the Commons were just as intractable from Charles's point of view in the provinces as in the capital. Parliament was dissolved, and a new one was convened for the autumn of 1680. Shaftesbury was determined to oppose the succession to the throne of the Catholic Duke of York and to give all his support to the Protestant Duke of Monmouth. The Earl of Halifax opposed Shaftesbury and spoke up for another Protestant, William of Orange. Locke was always at hand as Shaftesbury's faithful adviser, and in the troubled period that followed he went back and forth between London and Oxford spying out the land.

On March 21, 1681, the new Parliament met in Oxford. Shaftesbury and his Whig followers arrived burning with confidence and received a hearty welcome from the townsfolk. Locke was there and was busy negotiating the use of part of the house of John Wallis, his friend the great mathematician, for Shaftesbury during the meeting of Parliament. The session lasted for only a week, and

Locke, back in his rooms in Christ Church, was present for every moment of it. He was now in personal danger, for he was being secretly watched by members of that High Church party which had tried to thwart him at every step. Chief among these spies was the Librarian of Christ Church, Humphrey Prideaux, already mentioned in a pleasanter connection, who for the past eighteen months had been sending reports on Locke's activities to John Ellis, one of the under secretaries of state.

It soon became clear to Charles II that this Oxford Parliament was determined not to let him have his way, and, having managed to procure more money from Louis XIV, he dissolved it on March 28, 1681. Shaftesbury had failed. His fate was to be imprisonment in the Tower of London, acquittal, and flight to Holland, where he died early in 1683. After the dissolution of Parliament, Locke stayed on in Oxford until June: "the driest spring that hath been known," he recorded laconically, "there having been no rain from the end of March to the end of June."

He was in London on July 2, when Shaftesbury was arrested, but, being refused access to his patron, he returned to Oxford, and apart from a short stay in London again to be present at Shaftesbury's trial in November, he was in Oxford for the next eighteen months. They were anxious times for him, for he was now marked down as one of Shaftesbury's chief henchmen. Prideaux was not the only informer he had to fear. How close was the watch that was kept on Locke can be seen from this official report sent to Secretary of State Sir Leoline Jenkins on July 13, 1683:

"It is taken notice of in Oxford that from Mr. Locke's chamber in Christ Church, that was a great confident if not secretary, to the late Earl of Shaftesbury, in a clandestine way several handbaskets of papers are carried to Mr. James Tyrrell's house at Oakley, near Brill, in Buckinghamshire, about seven miles from Oxford, or to Mr Pawling's the mercer's, house in Oxford. Though Mr Tyrrell is son of a very good man, Sir Timothy Tyrrell, yet he and Mr Pawling are reported to be disaffected. It is thought convenient to make a search by a deputy lieutenant at Oakely, but who is Lieutenant or deputy of that county I cannot say, and if you at the same time direct a search by our Lord Lieutenant or one of his deputies at Mr Pawling's, and that the Bishop of Oxford and Vice-Chancellor then search Mr. Locke's chamber it may conduce to his Majesty's service. . . ."

Locke was by now convinced of his danger and began to make preparations to leave the country. In the summer of 1683 he destroyed many of his papers and handed over others to his trusted friend Edward Clarke, the husband of one of his Somerset cousins, with a long covering letter. About the same time he gave up keeping his diary in case it should be intercepted and perhaps used against him. Then, having just before posted a short note to Clarke telling him that he was about to sail for Rotterdam, he embarked secretly for the United Provinces, that haven of toleration. He arrived in Rotterdam during the first week of September.

He was never to reside in Oxford again. In November, 1684, John Fell, Dean of Christ Church received a letter

from the Earl of Sunderland in his capacity of Chief Secretary of State, asking for the removal from his senior
studentship of "one Mr Locke, who belonged to the late
Earl of Shaftesbury, and has upon several occasions be-
haved himself very factiously and undutifully to the government." Dr. Fell, although politically opposed to
Locke, was an honest man and seems to have been very
worried about what to do. He talked the matter over with
James Tyrrell and, according to Lady Masham, writing
many years later, "was so well satisfied of Mr Locke's
innocence that instead of obeying the order . . . he summoned him to return home . . . to answer for himself."

In the course of a lengthy letter to Sunderland, Dr.
Fell made the following observations:

"I have for diverse years had an eye upon him, but so
close has his guard been on himself, that after several
strict inquiries I may confidently affirm there is not any-
one in the college, however familiar with him, who has
heard him speak a word either against or so much as concerning the government; and although very frequently
both in public and in private, discourses have been purposely introduced to the disparagement of his master,
the Earl of Shaftesbury, his party and designs, he could
never be provoked to take any notice or discover in word
or look the least concern; so that I believe there is not in
the world such a master of taciturnity and passion.

"He has here a physician's place [a lay studentship],
which frees him from the exercises of the college, and the
obligations which others have to residence in it, and he
is now abroad upon want of health; but notwithstanding

that, I have summoned him to return home, which is done with this prospect, that if he comes not back he will be liable to expulsion for contumacy; if he does he will be answerable to your Lordship for what he shall be found to have done amiss; it being probable that though he may have been made thus cautious here, where he knew himself to be suspected, he has laid himself more open in London, where a general liberty of speaking was used, and where the execrable designs against his Majesty and his government were managed and pursued. . . ."

Fell's proposal was not accepted by the Court, and on November 16, 1684, Locke was expelled from Christ Church by royal command. He complained of his treatment in letters from Amsterdam to Dr. Fell and Lord Pembroke and pleaded innocence, but the decision of King Charles was irrevocable. Not till 1689, when, on the overthrow of James II, William of Orange was firmly installed as King, did Locke have any opportunity to win back his studentship. He then drafted a petition to have it restored to him, only to abandon the idea when, he said, he realised that it would mean turning out the innocent man who had been appointed in his place. That consideration may have been a mere excuse for not pursuing the matter further, for the truth of it was that Locke retained no particular interest in the University of Oxford. By then he had broken with his past, he had had experience of a wider world, his circle of friends had broadened, and all his energy was bent on his great philosophical undertakings. If he had ambition for an official position, that was to be found in London in working for the government, as he was soon to do as Commissioner for Trade. It is interesting to note that Sir Isaac Newton was similarly attracted to such matters; in the 1690's both turned from the academic field and became civil servants. The two geniuses met for the first time soon after Locke's return to England.

Thus he vanished from Oxford life in 1683, at which date the era of the University in the Age of Locke may be said to have ended. It had been a vivid and fruitful period, the culmination of the century of the new thought and the new science, which makes the seventeenth century in Europe the starting point of the Age of Enlightenment. Of that age, on the purely intellectual, if not on the scientific, side, Locke was certainly the parent.

Bibliographical Note

Invaluable above all for a study of Oxford during the second half of the seventeenth century is Anthony à Wood's *Life and Times* (5 vols., Oxford Historical Society, O.S. xix, xxi, xxvi, xxx, and xl). The Reverend Andrew Clark was the skilful editor of this work, which is a full transcription of Wood's diary and note-books.

From *Wood's City of Oxford* (O.H.S., O.S. xv) and *Oxford Council Acts, 1601–1700* (O.H.S., N.S. ii) one can reconstruct much of the City's history during this period.

C. E. Mallet's standard *History of the University of Oxford* (3 vols., 1924–27) contains a good section on seventeenth-century Oxford.

J. A. R. Marriott's *Oxford in National History* (1933)

contains some suggestive comments on the subject of Oxford in the setting of English politics.

R. T. Gunther's *Early Science at Oxford*, of which many volumes have been published by the Oxford Historical Society, is for all its dullness and barren style essential for a study of the subject, the first two volumes (O.H.S., O.S. lxxvii and lxxviii) being the two important ones for the general reader.

There is a worthwhile account of Locke's life at Oxford to be found in the first volume of H. R. Fox Bourne's *Life of John Locke* (2 vols., 1876), while in that rambling book, Christopher Wordsworth's *Social Life at the English Universities* (1874), there is some out-of-the-way information about seventeenth-century Oxford.

The Portfolio of Maps of Oxford (O.H.S., O.S. xxxviii) is of the greatest importance topographically.

Index